Before "I Do"

Before "I Do"

LEADERS' GUIDE

Anthony Garascia

Preparing for the
Sacrament of Marriage

ave maria press   Notre Dame, Indiana

Anthony Garascia currently serves as a pastoral minister and marriage and family therapist at St. Pius X Parish in Granger, Indiana. He holds an M.A. in Liturgical Studies from Catholic University and an M.S. in Counseling from Indiana University. In addition to his pastoral work, he serves as an adjunct faculty member in the theology department at the University of Notre Dame. His articles have appeared in numerous journals, including *Today's Parish*, *Living Light*, *Catechumenate*, and *Worship*.

Nihil obstat: Rev. Augustine DiNoia, O.P.; Mr. Fred Everett, Mrs. Lisa Everett; Rev. Jerome Listecki; Rev. Val Peter; Daniel Scheidt; Prof. Janet Smith; Rev. Peter

Imprimatur: Most Rev. John M. D'Arcy
                    Bishop of Fort Wayne-South Bend
                    November 1, 1998, Feast of All Saints

The *Imprimatur* is an official declaration that a book or pamphlet is free of doctrinal or moral error. No implication is contained therein that those who have granted the *Imprimatur* agree with its contents, opinions, or statements expressed.

Excerpts from *This Is Our Faith* by Michael Pennock © 1998 Ave Maria Press, used by permission. Excerpts from *The Church, Our Story* by Patricia Morrison Driedger © 1999 Ave Maria Press, used by permission.

International Standard Book Number: 0-87793-663-3

Cover and text design by Brian C. Conley

Printed and bound in the United States of America.

Library of Congress Cataloging-in-Publication Data
Garascia, Anthony
     Before "I do" : preparing for the sacrament of marriage : leader's guide / Anthony Garascia.
        p.   cm.
     Includes bibliographical references.
     ISBN 0-87793-663-3 (leader's guide)
     1. Marriage—Religious aspects—Catholic Church. 2. Marriage counseling.
     3. Catholic Church—Doctrines.   I. Title.
BX2250.G27   1998
259'.13—dc21   98-11841
                                                     CIP

I wish to express my appreciation to the following people:

Holly Taylor Coolman for her positive and insightful suggestions in the development of this work.

Bob Hamma, for his careful editing, helpful suggestions and encouraging presence, from the beginning and to the end of the process.

The people of St. Pius Tenth Church, Granger, Indiana, who have given me a home base in which to develop ideas while serving people in need.

Rev. Peter A. Jarret, C.S.C., who as pastor encouraged me to proceed with this work.

Contents

1

Getting Started

The Goals of This Program

Welcome to *Before "I Do,"* a program designed to assist priests, deacons, and a variety of pastoral ministers who collaborate in various ways in the proximate preparation of engaged couples for marriage. *Before "I Do"* is, first and foremost, a pastoral program. As such, it does not aim to provide a fully developed theology of marriage, or to make up for whatever may be missing in a couple's catechetical formation and understanding of the faith. It does, however, aim to be a resource to assist priests and other pastoral ministers whom the Rite of Marriage calls to "strengthen and nourish the faith of those who are about to be married, for the sacrament of marriage presupposes and demands faith."[1]

The introduction to the rite further specifies that the priest should offer the couple "a review of the fundamentals of Christian doctrine. This may include instruction on the teaching about marriage and the family, on the rites used in the celebration of the sacrament itself, and on the prayers and readings."[2] While the aim of this program is to assist in this process, it does not claim to be a comprehensive treatment of these issues. Because there will be a wide variety of levels of understanding of the fundamentals of Christian doctrine, the priest or deacon presiding at the wedding will need to assess the couple's need in this area. It is also presumed that the priest or deacon will engage the couple in the planning of the wedding liturgy. Numerous resources are available for liturgy planning, including *Together for Life* (also available from Ave Maria Press).

The principle aim of *Before "I Do"* is to help engaged couples prepare for the commitment and responsibilities that the sacrament of marriage entails. In his 1981 apostolic exhortation *On the Family*, Pope John Paul II called the Church to do just this:

> The Church must therefore promote better and more extensive programs of marriage preparation in order to eliminate as far as possible the difficulties that many married couples find themselves in, and even more to favor positively the establishing and maturing of successful marriages.[3]

The approach of this program is primarily pastoral. *Before "I Do"* attempts to tap into the excitement and enthusiasm already present in the engaged couple and to focus that energy into building a spiritual foundation for marriage, a foundation that will last. It seeks to constantly remind couples that marriage is more than the wedding, that it is a lived reality embedded in the mystery of the triune God who calls us to the fullness of life in Christ through the Holy Spirit.

Three aspects comprise this pastoral approach to marriage preparation. These three areas are built upon the latest research into the most effective marriage preparation programs. They are:

(1) Facilitation of Insight and Awareness

The program attempts to facilitate a process whereby the engaged couple gains insight into the influences that have shaped the two of them through the years, and how these influences affect the way they interact with each other in the present. Many engaged couples already come into marriage preparation with a good amount of energy and insight. In this case the task is to *validate and affirm* the energy and awareness already present in the engaged couples. However, as the saying goes, "love is blind;" engaged couples don't always see everything about how they interact and are often grateful when they learn something important about themselves in the course of their preparation.

(2) Relational Skills

Insight into oneself is often sufficient to initiate change and to foster a deeper commitment to the process of building a mature relationship. However, actual skill-building is also an essential component, especially in the areas of communication and conflict resolution. Many engaged and married couples have underdeveloped skills in this area or have learned unhealthy and harmful ways of communication from their families of origin. These unhealthy patterns can block the development of a mature relationship, and in the extreme lead to the downfall of the marriage.

(3) *Placing Spirituality as a Significant Component to Marriage Preparation*

This program is built around the belief that an understanding of and a commitment to grow in a Catholic Christian spirituality is essential for a lasting marriage. As a result, each of the six sessions in this program includes a section on the spirituality of marriage. Further, Sessions Two through Six begin with a reflection on some dimension of the sacramentality of marriage. A whole-hearted, positive embrace of the spirituality of Catholic marriage can be a positive and efficacious reality for the engaged couple. Too often we downplay the wisdom of our tradition because one of the engaged parties is a member of another Christian denomination, or because everyone involved is a little embarrassed to talk about their faith. As this discomfort fades, an engaged couple will begin to expect to talk about spirituality and will even miss this aspect if it is not included.

The Design of the Program

This program is written for two different types of implementation, the *couple-to-couple* approach and the *group preparation* approach. While both approaches have the same goals, their methodologies vary enough so as to call for separate implementation notes. Both approaches are given fuller treatment below.

Couple-to-Couple Approach

In this model, the engaged couple is assigned to a married couple in the parish or other pastoral setting (e.g., campus ministry, etc.). The married couple is often referred to as the *lead couple*, as this couple will take leadership in facilitating the interaction between the engaged couple and themselves. Once assigned, the lead couple makes contact with the engaged couple and sets up the first appointment or sessions.

Sessions are usually held in the lead couple's home, although they may sometimes be scheduled at a more neutral site like a parish office. The benefit of meeting in the lead couple's home is that the engaged couple gets to see first-hand the workings of an established household with all of its uniqueness. It can be important, for instance, for an engaged couple to witness firsthand how the lead couple handles things like bedtime for their own children.

11

Most couple-to-couple programs are four to six sessions in length, with individual sessions taking from ninety minutes to two hours. The benefits to this type of an approach are obvious: the engaged couple gets a one-on-one opportunity to reflect on how they have prepared for marriage thus far and an opportunity to continue the preparation over the next four to six sessions. The engaged couple also has the opportunity of learning from the experiences of the married couple. It often happens that many engaged couples develop close ties with their lead couple, and it is not unusual for them to stay in touch months and sometimes years after their wedding date.

The disadvantages of a couple-to-couple approach are few. The most serious drawback to this type of program occurs when either the right "chemistry" does not occur between the engaged and lead couple, or when one or both of the engaged couple comes into the program resistant or resentful at having to participate. These issues will be addressed in Chapter Four of this manual.

The Group Program

This approach calls for many engaged couples to come and participate in a program designed to provide both private and group reflection on the topic of marriage. In this approach, a *Marriage Preparation Team* usually takes responsibility for the planning and implementation of the day. Some members of the team may have specific responsibilities such as giving talks, while others may serve as facilitators of the small group reflection.

The length of the program varies with each program's objectives. Some programs cover eight to ten hours in a day or weekend, while others cover much more time over a series of gatherings. The second approach allows for more group process where engaged couples tell stories and get to meet other couples with similar interests and goals.

Some group programs include a presentation on a given topic by a guest speaker(s). Thus, if the topic for the evening is conflict it would be expected that someone—usually a married couple—would make a presentation on the topic. The presentation would cover two aspects: personal sharing on how the couple dealt with the topic in their own lives, and practical information concerning the topic. In the case of the topic of conflict, it would be expected that the participants would receive some information about how to handle conflict in their own relationship.

One of the benefits of a group program is the rapport that can develop between the engaged couples who participate in the program. In this setting, team members can intentionally plan opportunities for mixing and sharing between the couples with the expectation that interpersonal learning will occur. The fact that everyone is united around the common task of preparing for marriage also creates a sense of camaraderie that can be utilized by the team.

This approach can have shortcomings, especially if the team is too large and the leadership team does not have the necessary leadership skills. Then the group process will hinder, not facilitate, rapport between couples. Teams need especially to try to be aware of designing group processes that match the maturity and age level of the participants. While avoiding "gimmicks," group processes should invite participants into an ever-deepening sharing of their experience.

The Use of Pre-Marriage Inventories in a Marriage Prep Program

Research has shown that the most helpful marriage preparation involves a combination of "clergy, parish staff, and lay couples."[4] In this ideal form of marriage preparation each party involved assumes a distinct role. Most often the clergy will meet with a couple to begin the proximate preparation, which includes establishing general expectations for marriage preparation as well as specific expectations for the wedding itself. Either the clergy person himself or a staff person will usually administer a premarital inventory and schedule subsequent meetings to interpret the survey for the couple. As this process gets underway, the couple is then either referred to a parish program or a weekend experience such as Engaged Encounter.

Marriage preparation inventories are instruments that cover a comprehensive set of themes dealing with the skills required for a successful marriage. The themes include communication, extended family, interreligious marriages, conflict resolution, personality, and key problem areas such as substance abuse and physical abuse. Participants who take the inventories are most often asked to agree or disagree with various statements on a particular theme. For instance, one statement might read: "I am concerned about the amount of alcohol that my partner consumes." If both check "disagree" then that item would not be flagged for discussion, since this would not emerge as a problem area. If either partner checks "agree," that question would be flagged, and the pastoral minister who administered the inventory would most probably pursue this as an issue for discussion.

Pre-marital inventories are a good tool for identifying areas for special discussion. They also give the couple feedback concerning how similar each person is to the other on a wide range of issues. When the responses to the inventory indicate a high degree of similarity in the answers, without a lot of "flagged" issues, the couple is often affirmed in their degree of preparedness for marriage. When there is a high degree of dissimilarity in responses this can become an opportunity to raise specific issues of preparedness; sometimes the pastoral minister will refer the couple for counseling so that they can work out whatever unresolved issues are raised.

The pre-marital inventory can be seen as the first step in marriage preparation. It should normally precede the second step of attendance at either the parish's marriage prep program or one sponsored or approved by the diocese. In this second stage there is not as much opportunity to pursue specific questions and issues in depth. The use of an inventory and the experience of working with someone trained in interpreting it provides an opportunity to alert the couple to potential trouble areas that remain hidden from their view. The marriage prep program, on the other hand, allows for interpersonal sharing of stories and learning from other married couples the "way of marriage." Here, the task of the lead couple or team members is not to ferret out unresolved issues as much as to invite the engaged couple to enter into a stance of reflective sharing and listening that deepens the bond between them and gives them a different perspective on issues that may be important to sustaining their commitment.

2

The Various Ministries Involved in Marriage Preparation

In his encyclical entitled *On the Family* (*Familiaris Consortio*) Pope John Paul II states: "The person principally responsible in the diocese for the pastoral care of the family is the bishop."[5] He goes on to outline how the Church provides pastoral care for families as well as its role in the preparation of engaged couples for marriage. He outlines three distinct periods of preparation for marriage: remote preparation, involving the experience of living in a family that provides a living testimony to what a marriage is; proximate preparation, involving the ongoing religious education and formation of the person through the years leading to adulthood; and immediate preparation, involving the parish priest, marriage preparation program, music director (if available), parish wedding coordinator (if available) and other lay people who may assist the parish in its celebration of the sacrament of marriage.

Each diocese implements the Vatican's directives in different and distinct ways according to the particular needs of its people. Most often, since the bishop cannot personally become involved in the specific immediate preparation of every engaged couple, he has delegated this responsibility to his priests, who in turn enlist the help of the laity to assist in the preparation of an engaged couple.

The Role of the Priest or Deacon

The National Conference of Catholic Bishops have identified two principal areas of concern for the clergy person who is preparing a couple for marriage: that of discerning the *presence of faith* on the part of the couple approaching him for the sacrament, and that of determining that the couple is *ready and free to marry*.[6] The priest's or deacon's role is an essential one. He represents the bishop and has the responsibility to insure that a couple approaching the sacrament meet the criteria outlined by the Church for a valid reception of the sacrament.

In dioceses with a shortage of priests, the bishop may delegate these responsibilities to a permanent deacon. If this occurs the deacon is the person given official jurisdiction over how marriage preparation is to be implemented at the local parish. Other dioceses face the shortage of both priests and permanent deacons and may turn to a religious brother, sister, or lay person to serve in an "extraordinary" capacity as the parish administrator. In this case the religious brother, sister, or lay person is delegated by the bishop and serves at his request. This is why, throughout this manual, the phrase, "priest, deacon, or pastoral minister" is used. The term "pastoral minister" refers to a nonordained religious brother, sister, or lay person who has been officially delegated by the bishop to serve in a parish.

The Criteria of Faith

The issue of discerning whether faith is present seems, at first glance, a simple thing. Either you have faith or you don't. Yet, the pope and National Conference of Catholic Bishops recognize that faith exists on many different levels and may be manifested in a "seminal" or pre-conscious way.[7] Even a couple that appears to be marrying in the Church for only "social" reasons (a church wedding "looks good" to family) may indeed have the seeds of faith deeply implanted.

The role of the priest in this regard is not so much to challenge and refuse but to invite and be hospitable to the couple, encouraging their continued growth in faith and spirituality. In the end, the Church tends toward leniency in assessing the faith life of the engaged couple. The only time when a priest, deacon, or pastoral minister has a duty to refuse the sacrament of marriage is when "an engaged couple explicitly and formally reject what the Church intends to do in the marriage of baptized persons."[8]

Fr. Joseph Champlin sums up the church's attitude very well:

Priests, deacons, and pastoral ministers need to challenge, but not crush those who come to them seeking the sacraments and services of the church.

They need to be at one and the same time, both teachers and shepherds, simultaneously holding up the ideal, while reaching out to marginal Catholics.

They need to be prophets, proclaiming God's message with consistency, truth, and courage, yet searching for stray members with compassion, mercy, and forgiveness. In preaching the demands of justice and holiness, they need, above all, to be like their Master, the suffering servant Messiah, extremely careful not break the bruised reed or to snuff out the smoldering wick.[9]

Readiness and Freedom to Marry

The second clearly defined role of the priest, deacon, or pastoral minister is to assess the couple's readiness and freedom to marry. This is a serious obligation because the entire theology of the sacrament depends on the couple making an intentional decision to enter into a marriage in the way that the Church understands marriage. In order to enter into marriage a person must have the necessary emotional maturity and be free of any serious impediment that might compromise his or her freedom to bring about the marriage bond.

In his initial meetings with the couple the priest, deacon, or pastoral minister must be convinced that both parties are indeed free to marry: that there has been no previous bond of marriage, that the individuals are of sound mind (no serious psychological illnesses that might impede freedom), that they are not under undue pressure to marry (in the case of a pregnancy, for instance), and that they both possesses sufficient maturity to intentionally enter into the bond of marriage. This duty is taken seriously, even to the extent of an official "pre-nuptial investigation" whose only purpose is to determine a couple's freedom to marry.

The issue of psychological readiness or maturity is more difficult to assess than, for instance, an obvious impediment such as a previous marriage. The priest, deacon, or pastoral minister has available to him resources such as pre-marital inventories which will identify serious issues that might impede a person's ability to give free and irrevocable consent to the marriage. In the event that the priest makes a judgment that a person is not psychologically ready for marriage the National Conference of Catholic Bishops' guidelines make it clear that the sacrament of marriage can only be refused for as long as the cause for refusal exists.

> The Revised Code of Canon Law . . . decrees that all persons not prohibited by law can contract marriage. . . . It does, nevertheless, empower the local ordinary to prohibit a person's marriage, but only for a time and for a serious cause—for as long as the cause exists. Dioceses with a common policy of selective postponement for the ill-prepared cite this empowerment as the legal basis for such a procedure.[10]

For instance, in the case of a person who experiences a serious depressive illness, a priest might recommend postponement of the marriage until the affected party has received sufficient treatment. Once treatment has demonstrated that this is no longer an impediment to a free consent, then the marriage can take place.

The Purposes of Marriage

There is one further role that the priest, deacon, or pastoral minister assumes: insuring that the couple, in making their vows, is entering into a marriage that conforms to the Church's teaching regarding the twofold meaning of marriage—mutual and lasting fidelity between the spouses and the procreation of children. The pre-nuptial investigation includes questions that cover a person's intention to enter a permanent marriage that can be dissolved only by death and an understanding that one purpose of marriage is the begetting and rearing of children.[11] Here, if a couple answers "no" to either of these questions, the priest, deacon, or pastoral minister is bound to refuse the sacrament because no marriage, in fact, can take place.

It also falls to the priest, deacon, or pastoral minister to raise with the engaged couple the issue of family planning. The National Conference of Catholic Bishops have stressed that marriage preparation should include teaching and information on responsible family planning, including guidance to the couple on what it means to form a mature conscience. Their criteria for a mature conscience involves attitudes of generosity, trust, humility, and mutuality, and decisions based on the wisdom and guidance of the Church.[12] They also emphasize that natural methods of family planning are the only methods approved by the Church. Many dioceses encourage engaged couples to attend a Natural Family Planning workshop before their marriage so that they can learn more about the advantages of choosing this method of family planning.

As expressed in the encyclical letter *On Human Life* (*Humane Vitae*) in 1968, the Church's teaching on the issue of artificial contraception is clear. Unfortunately, many couples view the Church's teaching on this issue as a judgment on them rather than as an invitation. The Church's teaching on this issue has a very real pastoral dimension, offering assistance and guidance to couples, many of whom are not fully aware of the values the Church's teaching on this subject upholds.

It must be emphasized, when all is said and done, that the Church holds that a baptized person has a right to the sacrament of marriage. Poorly developed faith, getting married for "cultural reasons," and other mixed motives are not in themselves reasons to deny a person the sacrament. As the National Conference of Catholic Bishops have stated: "The faith of the person seeking marriage in the Church can exist in varying degrees. It is the primary duty of pastors to facilitate a rediscovery of this faith, nourishing it and bringing it to maturity."[13]

The Role of the Marriage Preparation Program

Marriage preparation programs are an important help to the engaged couple's immediate preparation for marriage, but in themselves they are not essential to an engaged couple's readiness to marry. What this means is this: a priest, deacon, or pastoral minister doesn't send an engaged couple to a marriage prep program in order to assess their readiness to marry. Rather, he first assesses their readiness, and if he judges that they are ready to marry, sends them on to a marriage prep program so that they can be better prepared. We must be careful in assigning too great expectations and/or importance to marriage preparation programs. On the one hand, they are an important tool in assisting the couple to deepen their love, faith, and preparation for marriage. On the other hand, we shouldn't expect them to fully catechize a couple in the theology of marriage or be an evaluative tool whereby we try to "test" the readiness of a couple. They simply assist the Church in preparation of a couple, preparation that has already begun well before a couple approaches the Church.

The National Conference of Catholic Bishops reflected on the balance between a couple's readiness, faith development, and the role of marriage preparation programs:

> Pope John Paul II places this delicate issue of the engaged couple's faith and readiness in perspective when he both urges better and more intense programs of marriage preparation and stresses their necessity and obligation, yet cautions that omitting them is not an impediment to the celebration of marriage.[14]

Then why have a marriage prep program in the first place? Because research has shown that 50% of marriages that fail will fail within the first seven years of marriage, it makes sense to do whatever we can to bolster the readiness of a couple so that they can weather the inevitable strains that will test their relationship. Also, the fact that the local church expends so much time and energy in helping a couple prepare for marriage paves the way for a positive future relationship not only with the parish where the marriage is celebrated, but with any parish where the couple may live in the future. Given a good experience in marriage prep, a young married couple might be more inclined to turn to the Church should their marriage experience turbulence in the early years.

Research has indicated that the best form of marriage preparation is that of a team format. A study done by the Center for Marriage and Family at Creighton University stated:

> Marriage preparation is perceived as most valuable when it is administered by a team. Clergy working alone with a couple continues to be the most common format for administering marriage preparation, and it is perceived as a valuable format. In this study, however, respondents perceived it as a significantly less valuable format than administration by a team. A team make-up of clergy, lay couples, and parish staff was the instructor combination that yielded the highest perceived values. To be noted here is the critical role of clergy on this team. Respondents judged the absence of clergy from the marriage preparation process to be seriously detrimental to the process.[15]

It would appear, therefore, that a combination of clergy and lay involvement in the marriage preparation process is one of the most important things a parish can do for its engaged couples. The priest or deacon usually presents the Church's teachings on marriage and gives official sanction to the decision of an engaged couple to seek marriage in the first place. The laity on the team serve as witnesses to the qualities of faith, fidelity, and the other virtues that go into forming a successful and long-standing marriage. They also witness to the practical, day-to-day issues in developing a spirituality of marriage.

This marriage preparation program seeks to foster the ideal outlined above whereby a team comprised of clergy and laity work together to ensure the best possible preparation of an engaged couple. In this model there are clearly defined roles: the priest, deacon, or pastoral minister assumes responsibility for giving ecclesial affirmation of the couple and for imparting the essentials of the Church teaching on marriage. The lay people involved assist in the formation by their witness and by taking the engaged couple through a program aimed at skill-building and insight awareness. The engaged couple's book is meant to address only the lay role in the marriage preparation process. It does not seek to present a complete catechesis on the sacrament of marriage and presumes that such a teaching will be presented by the priest, deacon, or pastoral minister in accordance with his assessment of the couple's needs.

The participant's book is more oriented to practical skill-building and awareness while encouraging the participants to take seriously the deepening of their spirituality. It is not meant to be a course on either the theology or spirituality of marriage, although from time to time certain theological and spiritual issues may be raised for consideration by the couple.

The Role of the Music Director and/or Wedding Coordinator

Many parishes today employ a music director who is responsible for organizing the music wedding repertoire. This person will most probably meet with the engaged couple to begin the initial planning of the wedding liturgy and to select the music for the wedding. Many parishes are subject to their local diocese's guidelines on music for weddings. Thus, one role of the music director may be to exercise a veto over some music that might be requested during the service. Often, there will be a brochure or small booklet made available to the engaged couple as soon as they schedule their wedding, so that problems can be anticipated early and planned for. Some engaged couples don't understand the reasons why some of their songs are rejected, and it behooves the music director to have a well-thought-out policy that can be easily explained to a couple planning a wedding.

In some parishes there is a wedding coordinator who serves as the overall coordinator of parish ministries to the engaged. In large parishes this relieves the priest of a lot of important but non-essential work. For instance, if there is a booklet to be typed up which gives the order of service, the wedding coordinator would become involved. Also, in large parishes that might have two to three weddings a week, a wedding coordinator can insure that each party understands basic things like where to dress, when to arrive, how much time they have for pictures after the wedding, and when they need to leave the church so that the next party can begin its immediate preparations for the liturgy.

Other Professionals

Another valuable service to parishes today is that of the professional counselor who is experienced in relationship counseling and who may have a particular specialty in working with engaged couples. Often, the local Catholic Charities office works closely with parishes to provide services of this type. Also, there are usually available local therapists and/or counselors who specialize in this field and who are sympathetic to the goals and values of the Church in preparing couples for marriage. These professionals can be very helpful to the marriage preparation team, especially when there is an issue concerning readiness for marriage.

3

Understanding the Sacrament of Marriage

While the role of the mentor or team couples in a marriage preparation program is not to provide religious education for the engaged concerning the Church's theology of marriage, married couples sometimes find that as the level of trust and comfort grows, the engaged couple will raise questions in this area. The aim of this section is to offer married couples some background so that they may be better able to reflect the Church's vision of marriage in their sharing with the engaged. There may be times when it will be helpful to suggest that the engaged couple discuss their questions and concerns with the priest or deacon presiding at their wedding, yet there will be other occasions when married couples, because of their lived experience, can indeed be the best teachers of the faith.

The material in the first section of this chapter is excerpted from a widely used catechism *This Is Our Faith* by Michael Pennock.[16] The book has been recently revised to follow closely the *Catechism of the Catholic Church*. The second section of this chapter, "A Sacred Covenant, a Holy Sacrament," is the author's own theological reflection on marriage in light of Vatican II and the revised Rite of Marriage issued after the Council. Finally, a brief history of how marriage has been celebrated in the Catholic Church is offered. This material is excerpted from a recently published textbook, on *The Church: Our Story* by Pamela Driedger.[17]

Marriage: What the Church Teaches and Believes

What Is the Sacrament of Matrimony? [CCC 1601; 1660]

In the sacrament of matrimony a baptized man and woman vow their love in an exclusive, permanent, sexual partnership. This union is marked by love, respect, care, and concern, and a commitment to share responsibility in the raising of a family if God should bless them with children.

> The matrimonial covenant, by which a man and a woman establish between themselves a partnership of the whole of life, is by its nature ordered toward the good of the spouses and the procreation and the education of offspring; this covenant between baptized persons has been raised by Christ the Lord to the dignity of a sacrament.

> For this reason, a matrimonial contract cannot validly exist between baptized persons unless it is also a sacrament by that fact (Canon 1055).

Christian marriage is an extraordinary sign of God working through and in the ordinary. Christ Jesus has raised marriage to the dignity of a sacrament. Simply put, a good marriage is not only like a *civil contract* between two persons, rather, but also a holy covenant involving three persons. The couple is joined on their life's journey by Jesus Christ who promises to bless, sustain, and rejoice in their union.

What Does the Old Testament Say About Marriage? [CCC 1602-1608]

The vocation of marriage is written in the very nature of men and women who are created by a God of infinite love. Original sin, however, taints God's intent for the harmonious loving between men and women. Thus, men and women must seek God's grace to achieve the loving unity God intends for them.

Through the period of the original Covenant, there was a gradual growth in understanding of the meaning of marriage. In early times polygamy was tolerated; husbands could freely divorce their wives (who were often treated as property). By the time the book of Genesis was written, however, God revealed to the Jewish people two profound truths about the *purposes* of marriage. First, marriage is a share in God's creative purpose of bringing new life into the world. Second, marriage creates a new relationship—one that was not there before—between a husband and wife.

Genesis tells us that Yahweh established marriage and sex and declared that they are good and are meant for the procreation of human life.

> God created man in the image of himself,
> in the image of God he created him,
> male and female he created them.
> God blessed them, saying to them,
> "Be fruitful, multiply, fill the earth and subdue it. . . ."
> God saw all that he had made,
> and indeed it was very good (Gn 1:27-28, 31).

Genesis also reveals the other major purpose of marriage: companionship between friends who share the same life and love:

> This one at last is bone of my bones and flesh of my flesh!
> She is to be called Woman,
> because she was taken from Man.
> That is why a man leaves his father and mother
> and becomes attached to his wife,
> and they become one flesh (Gn 2:23-24).

God fully intends a permanent, exclusive, monogamous relationship between man and woman who have been created in the divine image.

How Does Marriage Mirror God's Love for Us? [CCC 1609-1611]

Divine mercy would not allow God to forsake humans tainted by sin. Although pain in childbirth and the need to toil by "the sweat of your brow" were two effects of original sin, God uses marriage to help man and woman "to overcome self-absorption, egoism, pursuit of one's own pleasure, and to open oneself to the other, to mutual aid and to self-giving" (CCC 1609).

The prophets use marriage as an image to describe Yahweh's great love for his people, Israel.

> I shall betroth you to myself for ever,
> I shall betroth you in uprightness and justice,
> and faithful love and tenderness (Hos 2:21).

The prophet Malachi forcefully states the ideal:

> Yahweh stands as witness between you and the wife of
> your youth, with whom you have broken faith, even

though she was your partner and your wife by covenant. Did he not create a single being, having flesh and the breath of life? (Mal 2:14-15).

Proverbs paints a picture of an ideal wife: "She is clothed in strength and dignity" (Prv 31:25). The books of Ruth and Tobit highlight the fidelity and tenderness of spouses. The Song of Songs describes love between a bride and a bridegroom. Because God has blessed marriage, affectionate, erotic love between a husband and wife is something good and holy and joyful.

What Does the New Testament Reveal About Marriage? [CCC 1613-1616; 1659]

The New Testament reveals further important insights into the nature of marriage. Jesus' attendance at the wedding feast of Cana underscores the goodness and naturalness of marriage. When Jesus teaches about marriage, he reaffirms the original intention of his Father—that marriage should be a permanent, exclusive love relationship:

> "Everyone who divorces his wife and marries another is guilty of adultery, and the man who marries a woman divorced by her husband commits adultery" (Lk 16:18).

Jesus shows his profound respect for human dignity when he teaches that looking at a woman lustfully is the equivalent of committing adultery (Mt 5:27-28). Motives and interior attitudes are important to him.

The early church also regarded marriage highly. St. Paul, for example, supplies a key teaching on marriage:

> In the same way, husbands must love their wives as they love their own bodies; for a man to love his wife is for him to love himself. A man never hates his own body, but he feeds it and looks after it; and that is the way Christ treats the Church, because we are parts of his Body. . . . This mystery has great significance, but I am applying it to Christ and the Church (Eph 5:28-32).

The union of a husband and wife is like the union of Christ with his church. St. Paul calls this reality a *mystery* (a word translated by St. Augustine as "sacrament"). Christian marriage is an external sign of Christ's love. Marriage is a covenant, a total lifelong commitment that mirrors Christ's love for his church.

How Is Marriage a Covenant? [CCC 1612; 1617; 1661]

The church teaches us that the sacrament of marriage mirrors God's covenant of love with his people. By giving us his Son, the Father loves us freely and faithfully keeps his promises to us. Jesus—the greatest sign of God's love—draws us into community, showers us with unexpected gifts, relates to us as unique individuals, and invites us to grow in love by serving others.

In the covenant of Christian marriage, a husband and wife freely bind themselves together for life. Theirs is an open-ended commitment to love exclusively. No time conditions or any other conditions are put on their relationship. In sickness or health, in poverty or wealth, in good times and in bad times, the couple promises to be faithful. A marriage covenant commitment mirrors God's unconditional love for his people. If a man and woman insist on certain conditions when getting married, they are simply engaged in a legal contract.

In Christian marriage love is freely given and faithfully weathers the trials that come its way. Christian marriage is life-giving because through it God gives the married couple the privilege of procreating life.

It is full of surprises, providing countless opportunities to grow in holiness.

It is a concrete way to live the Christian life of love and service in the context of family living.

It is a place to receive the Lord who showers the couple with the graces to love each other with the very love he has for the church. These graces perfect the human love of the spouses, strengthen their indissoluble unity, and sanctify them on their journey to eternal life.

How Is the Sacrament of Matrimony Celebrated? *[CCC 1621-1624; 1663]*

In the Christian marriage, the spouses are the ministers of the sacrament. They mutually confer the sacrament on one another by exchanging marriage vows before the Church. The sacrament of Christian marriage usually takes place during a eucharistic celebration. By having a wedding with Mass, the couple celebrates their spousal love as a reflection of the sacrificial love that the Lord has for the couple and the church. Also, because the couple about to be married should be worthy to receive the sacrament of marriage fruitfully, the church recommends that the couple prepare for it by confessing their sins in the sacrament of reconciliation beforehand.

The wedding liturgy includes an entrance procession, greeting, prayers, readings, and homily. After this, the priest questions the couple concerning their freedom in choosing marriage, their desire to be faithful, and their willingness to have and rear children. The bridal couple then exchanges vows in the presence of the priest, two witnesses, and the assembled Christian community. The groom and bride join hands and in turn verbalize their consent. They promise to be true in good times and bad, in sickness and in health, and to love and honor each other until death.

As the church's official witness, the priest blesses the rings and asks the couple to exchange them as symbols of fidelity and unending love. The liturgy of the Eucharist proceeds as usual with the nuptial blessing given after the Lord's Prayer.

When a man and woman exchange their vows, the church witnesses, blesses, and celebrates their covenant promises. However, the sacrament of marriage is not just a one-day affair; it unfolds over the years as the husband and wife live out their mutual relationship with each other and the Lord. The risen Lord promises to be with the couple to sustain them on their life journey. He sanctifies sexual love, a most powerful sign of total, exclusive, intimate sharing. He sustains the couple in the ordinary give-and-take of family life. He empowers them to be signs of love to each other, their children, and to all their friends and acquaintances. Through their daily love and fidelity, they will meet the Lord who lives within them by the power of the Holy Spirit. The celebration of Christian marriage is "till death do us part."

What Are the Requirements for a Valid Marriage? [CCC 1625-1631; 1662]

To celebrate the sacrament of marriage validly, the couple must be of mature age, unmarried, not closely related by blood or marriage, and they must freely consent to marry. Freedom of consent means that neither party is under constraint nor impeded by any natural or church law.

The exchange of consent is the indispensable element that makes the marriage valid. This consent, in which the parties freely give themselves to each other, must be free of coercion or grave external fear. If freedom is lacking, then the marriage never really exists.

Consent means that a couple commits themselves to a lifelong covenant of love. Furthermore, the spouses must be capable of sharing sexually since sexual intercourse is a sign of mutual love and union, the full expression of the mutual love between husband and wife. Finally, the couple must be open to the possibility of raising a family if God blesses the marriage with children.

In the Christian marriage, the ministers of the sacrament of Christian marriage are the bride and bridegroom themselves. Because marriage is an ecclesial reality, church law requires that a Catholic couple exchange their vows before a priest and two other witnesses. Exchanging vows publicly helps the spouses remain faithful to their commitments.

How Does a Couple Prepare for Marriage? [CCC 1632-1637]

Marriage is important not only to the couple but to the church and society as a whole. For this reason, the church puts a great emphasis on suitable marriage preparations. The witness of loving parents and families is critical, but so are the catechetical efforts of pastors and the parish community.

Preparation for a Christian marriage in most dioceses includes a requirement that the engaged couple participate in a marriage preparation conference, retreat, or workshop. These church-sponsored "classes" give the couple an opportunity to learn about what the sacramental commitment entails from a priest and members of the community, including couples who are living the sacrament. During the period of preparation, a priest or other parish minister will continue to meet with the couple to prepare them for the serious commitment they are about to make. Topics examined in these meetings include communication skills, parenting issues, the role of a faith life in marriage, and plans for the actual ceremony.

When a Catholic marries a non-Catholic Christian (a mixed marriage), special attention is paid to the situation by the couple and the pastor. When a Catholic marries a non-baptized person, an express dispensation must be granted for the marriage to be valid. The Catholic partner promises to continue to live his or her Catholic faith and have his or her children baptized and raised in the Catholic faith. The non-Catholic partner is made aware of this pledge, but is not required to make any promises. Both partners must know and not exclude the essential purposes and qualities of marriage, and the non-Catholic partner must not exclude the promise of the Catholic partner.

The banns (announcements) of marriage are usually printed in the parish bulletin for three consecutive weeks before the wedding ceremony. The reason for the publication and reading of the banns is to notify the Christian community of the impending celebration and to give informed parties the opportunity to come forward if they know any reason the sacrament of marriage should not take place.

When one of the parties is a non-Catholic, special permission can be obtained from the local bishop and pastor for a minister of another faith to participate in the marriage ceremony. In extraordinary circumstances a dispensation might be given for a minister of another faith to witness the exchange of vows.

What Is an Annulment? [CCC 1629]

An annulment is an official declaration of the Catholic church that what appeared to be a valid Christian marriage in fact was not. A couple may have entered the marriage psychologically immature or lacking true understanding of the demands a marriage covenant makes. One or both partners might not have given free, true consent to the marriage. Perhaps one or both partners intended never to have children. Possibly one or both partners were incapable of sexual relations.

A "failed" marriage may never have been a true Christian marriage to begin with. In these cases the couple should submit their situation to the diocesan marriage tribunal (court) for examination and judgment. If it can be shown that the marriage was not valid from the beginning, then the individuals involved are free to enter a true Christian marriage in the future.

What Are the Principal Effects of the Sacrament of Matrimony? [CCC 1638-1642]

Christ's love sanctifies the love of the husband and wife in the sacrament of marriage. Once the marriage is consummated, an irrevocable, perpetual, and exclusive bond results between the spouses who freely consented to become lifelong partners. Their relationship is covenantal, not simply contractual, in which the Lord showers his graces to perfect their love and strengthen their unity. A major fruit of their life in common is the welcoming of any children God may send them. Their life together, along with their efforts to rear and educate their children in a family setting, is the primary means for a married couple to attain holiness.

What Are the Essential Qualities of a Christian Marriage? [CCC 1643-1645; 1652-1654; 1664]

Christian marriage involves a total commitment of a couple's bodies, feelings, affections, hearts, wills, and spirits. It results in a deep unity of body, heart, and soul. As a result, marriage demands indissolubility, fidelity, and openness to fertility. Practices contrary to these essential goods include polygamy, which destroys the exclusivity of marriage and undermines the dignity of the man and woman; divorce, which ends up separating what God has joined together; and refusal of fertility (i.e., artificial contraception or abortion), which deflects marriage from its greatest gift—children.

Married love is a great gift from God. Sexual sharing in a marriage is a profound means of love and commitment between a man and a woman. Its purpose in God's plan is twofold: *unitive*, that is, to bond a man and woman together as partners for life; and *procreative*, that is, to share in God's creative activity of bringing new life into the world. Children are the crowning gifts of marriage, contributing to the good of the mother and father. Marriage and the family are the exemplars of God's gift of life and are at the service of life.

Why Is Christian Marriage a Permanent Commitment? [CCC 1646-1651; 1665]

The example of permanent marriage commitment is a prime way to bring Christ into the world. This is concretely true for the children who result from the marriage. Children first encounter the love and knowledge of God from their parents and are, in fact, living symbols of their parents' love. Children need the stable, reassuring love of a solid marriage to develop healthy attitudes to life and to God.

But a faithful marriage is a powerful sign to those outside of the immediate family as well. Just as God's love is unconditional and eternal, so the Christian husband and wife strive for this ideal in their lives together. Their fidelity and exclusive love is an extraordinary sign to the world of God's fidelity and undying love for his people.

Jesus himself underscored the permanence of the marriage bond:

> "Have you not read that the Creator from the beginning *made them male and female* and that he said: *This is why a man leaves his father and mother and becomes attached to his wife, and the two become one flesh?* They are no longer two, therefore, but one flesh. So then, what God has united, human beings must not divide" (Mt 19:4-6).

Thus the Catholic church does not permit divorce and remarriage because Jesus forbade it. The covenant made between two validly married Catholics can only be dissolved by the death of one of the partners. In extraordinary circumstances a couple may separate for the good of the children and the individuals involved. Though the civil authority may dissolve the legal aspects of a valid marriage (called in civil law a divorce), the state has no authority to dissolve a true Christian marriage—its true sacramental nature.

According to church teaching, a legally separated Catholic (divorced under civil law) may not remarry while his or her spouse is alive. This teaching is consistent with the Lord's teaching, "Everyone who divorces his wife and marries another is guilty of adultery" (Lk 16:18). Christ calls his disciples to high standards. Moreover, he gives them the grace to live his commands. The church encourages a person who is suffering from a broken marriage to continue to celebrate the sacraments and remain close to the Christian community. The Lord promises in a special way to bless those who suffer most. Fellow Christians should support hurting brothers and sisters, pray for them, and help them to "live out their situation in a Christian manner" (CCC 1649).

A Sacred Covenant, a Holy Sacrament

Since the close of the Second Vatican Council the Church has placed greater emphasis on marriage as covenant while also re-emphasizing marriage as a sacrament. The first two paragraphs of the Introduction to the Rite of Marriage state:

> 1. In virtue of the sacrament of marriage, married Christians signify and share in the mystery of the unity and fruitful love that exists between Christ and his Church; they thus help each other to attain holiness in their married life and in welcoming and rearing children and they have their own special place and gift among the people of God.

> 2. A marriage is established by the marriage covenant, the irrevocable consent that the spouses freely give to and receive from each other. This unique union of a man and a woman and the good of the children impose total fidelity on each of them and the unbreakable unity of their bond. . . . [18]

The notion of a covenant relationship dates back to ancient Israel, before the time of King David. It was a secular term borrowed by the writers of the Jewish scriptures to describe the relationship that God had with his people Israel. In the secular meaning, a covenant was a specific relationship entered into by two unequal parties, usually states. The weaker party sought protection from the more powerful party and agreed to the terms laid out for it by its powerful ally. For its part the more powerful party agreed to offer protection to the weaker party.

The application to the relationship between God and the people of Israel becomes clear when cast in the above light of a covenant relationship. Israel was in need of a protector, as it was often a pawn in the maneuverings of nation states like Assyria, Babylon, and Egypt. The God of Israel, after the giving of the Ten Commandments, became Israel's protector and promised to always be faithful to the people of Israel. For its part, Israel agreed to abide by the commandments outlined in the decalogue.

As the history of Israel unfolded, later prophets would emphasize the relational aspect of the covenant between Israel and her God. It was a natural development to compare God's love for his people to that of a bridegroom for his bride. God was said to have "nuptial" love for his people.

In the New Covenant inaugurated by Jesus the image of a wedding looms large in understanding God's love for his people. Jesus' presence and actions at the wedding feast at Cana (Jn 2:1-11) establish the sacramental quality of marriage. This event also expands the image of the wedding feast, promoted by the prophets, as a foretelling of the messianic banquet.

In speaking of marriage the *Catechism of the Catholic Church* talks about the "spousal love" between Christ and the Church.[19] Marriage as a sacrament points toward the love between Christ and the Church, and offers the grace to make present his love in the concrete ways that the two married people live their life together. We say that sacraments are efficacious signs, meaning that they bring about what is signified. If marriage points toward the hidden reality of Christ's love for the Church, then in a Christian marriage the couple creates that same love in their own personal way.

But there is another important but less obvious point to be made about the covenant relationship of marriage. That is that the two married people, in taking on the responsibility to be a sign of Christ's love for the Church, willingly bring about an irrevocable bond, a permanent bond. This is because their very commitment points toward the unfailingly, permanent love of God, and because a sacrament brings about what it signifies, the bond entered into by two married people creates the same type of bond as the bond between God and his people: permanent and lasting.

There is a bit of a contradiction here that has to do with the fact that we experience ourselves as sinners called to holiness. It is this: how can two people, with all of their inadequacies and frailties, dare to call into existence a bond that is like that between God and his people, and one that is permanent and lasting? Can any of us guarantee fidelity like that which God has for his people? We would be fools if we said we could. In raising marriage to a sacramental level it would seem that Jesus is asking perhaps too much of a married couple.

The answer to this dilemma is to be found in the original notion of a covenant relationship. Israel was the weaker, sinful party to the covenant with God. God knew that Israel as a nation would flounder and wander away from him, yet continued to renew the covenant with Israel again and again. Because it was a permanent bond, the relationship was, and is, permanent. In other words, no matter what Israel did to harm the covenant, it was God who was always faithful, always calling Israel to a deeper holiness.

The same is true for the sacrament of marriage. In a sense, the two people who marry each other represent or symbolize the Church and the entire people of God. The two people making their vows together can be said to represent Israel before Mount Sinai, ready to receive their terms of the covenant, the ten commandments. In other words, marriage as a sacrament is not a solitary act between two people. Rather, a sacramental marriage in the Catholic Church begins when two baptized Christians make vows together in the presence of a minister of the Church. The ecclesial community, which also includes relatives, friends, and acquaintances, gives acceptance of, and witness to, a new social unit which is the foundation of family life within the Christian community. Not only does marriage spring from the community, it creates it as well. With the arrival of children, the Christian family becomes the Church on the most local level.

The other notion to ponder is the fact that just as the Church is comprised of sinners called to holiness, so the two newly married spouses embark on a journey of holiness where they will be called to confront the harmful aspects of their own sinfulness. This journey is a journey towards holiness and wholeness. Just as God knew beforehand that Israel could fail its part of the covenant, yet was always present and faithful to Israel, we too can trust that God will be faithful to two people who could falter in their permanent bond by their fallible conduct.

In the end perhaps the most important thing about the aspect of covenant is that it speaks of an ongoing, lasting relationship between God and the two married people. Placing the emphasis on relationship calls for a more dynamic process that moves beyond the legalities of civil and church laws to a relationship that relies on the living, loving God to sustain the core of their commitment.

A Brief History of the Marriage Rite

In the first century marriage rites presumably followed Jewish and pagan customs with the elimination of anything that was explicitly objectionable to Christians. The majority of marriages took place in the home and were private celebrations that did not require the presence of Church leaders. A marriage contract was publicly agreed upon by both families. The groom and the veiled bride were brought together and blessed, and then everyone feasted. The blessing of the couple was usually given by a family member, often the bride's father. Late in the first century Ignatius, the bishop of Antioch, said that it was better if Christians married with the approval of the local bishop so that "their marriage may be according to the Lord, and not after their own lust." He did not, however, suggest any particular ritual for a Christian marriage.

Over the next few centuries certain specifically Christian customs developed for weddings. The marriage blessing began to take on a definite liturgical structure and there was an increasing reluctance to marry during Advent or Lent. In some places a celebration of the Eucharist followed the blessing of the couple, and on occasion the Eucharist actually replaced the traditional wedding feast.

The primary image of marriage through the first millennium was that of a contract. In the middle ages the porch of the church became the place where legal contracts were ratified before God and before the community; therefore, marriages gradually moved from the home to the porch of the

34

church. The pressure to have marriages take place in the church grew stronger as the need grew for written documentation to prove legitimate births and the right of inheritance. Priests were the only people in most villages who could read and write; therefore, it became necessary to have them present at the wedding. It was only around the sixteenth century that all marriages moved into the church and that the celebration of a Nuptial Mass became the norm.

Wedding vows had to be pronounced both freely and in public. Thus they became the first liturgical texts in the language of the people rather than in Latin. Wedding vows themselves have changed very little over the centuries. The *Manual of York Use,* written in the fourteenth century, contains the following vow: "Here I take you [name] to my wedded wife, to hold and to have at bed and at board, for fairer for fouler, for better for worse, in sickness and in health, till death us do part, if holy Church it will ordain, and thereto I plight you my troth."

One of the major changes in the wedding ceremony since Vatican II has been the stress on the equality of the marriage partners. The pre-Vatican II rite included a prayer for the bride that she be "faithful to one embrace . . . honorable in her chastity." There was no similar prayer for the groom. The post-Vatican II rite contains no such inequalities.

4

Special Pastoral Issues

Interreligious or "Mixed Marriages"

Recent statistics indicate that about forty percent of American Catholics marry someone from a different religious affiliation.[20] What this means for those conducting a marriage prep program is that traditional and familiar religious language and concepts cannot be presumed.

Religious differences can also be a source of conflict in a marriage, especially if the question of the religious upbringing of children is unresolved.[21] Thus, it behooves the couple to discuss openly their expectations concerning how it is they will resolve this potential source of tension.

The influence of the marriage prep program in assisting engaged couples to think through the differences in their religious views and/or practices should not be underestimated. Lead couples and team members can go a long way toward modeling acceptance of differences and enthusiasm for making spirituality a significant aspect of the early married commitment.

When working with a couple in this situation keep in mind the following:

1. Don't apologize for your own faith. A person from another religious tradition might come to the sessions with a mixture of curiosity and indifference. If he or she witnesses team members and lead couples downplaying their own Catholic experience then this person could form the impression that Catholicism is not very important.

2. Don't oversell the Catholic experience either. Know your faith and be comfortable in expressing how it "works" for you by solving the bigger problems of meaning and belonging in your life. Keep in mind that you are modeling a certain way of being religious even though you might not be intentional about it.

3. Be ready to give good reasons why anyone might be interested in exploring Catholicism. A marriage prep program can be looked at as another way of evangelizing, that is, bringing the good news to people. If there are any inquiries about the Catholic Church, be ready to refer to the local parish's catechumenate program. A young couple who participates in this type of program receives, in many respects, the best form of preparation for marriage.

4. Without trying to scare the couple, be ready to discuss with them the facts of interreligious marriages. Research has shown that in fifty percent of these marriages one spouse converts to the other's religion; that the mother has a stronger influence on the children's religious identification, but that the father's participation is important for the religious development of sons; and that there is a slightly higher divorce rate in interreligious marriages.[22]

5. Regardless of the question of where the two will worship, stress with the couple the importance of developing a spirituality of marriage. This involves, in part, an attitude that our lives are interconnected in a web of communities, that all humans share a common bond, and that a transcendent force is somehow at work in the cosmos and in our lives. Ask the couple to seriously consider how it is they intend to ritualize the important aspects of their lives, and whether religion and spirituality have any place in that task.

Cohabitation

Engaged couples living together before marriage present a unique and significant pastoral challenge to anyone involved in the ministry of marriage preparation. It is not uncommon for pastors and pastoral ministers to encounter fifty percent of couples seeking marriage in the Church to be already living together under one roof.

The National Conference of Catholic Bishops define cohabitation as a couple who have been living together at least four nights a week for an extended period of time, where a commitment to each other exists, and where there is some recognition that the couple form a family or household.[23] Many people do not use the term "cohabitation" but use the term "living together" to describe a situation where there is a commitment to share economic and household resources, and where the commitment includes a serious level of emotional and sexual sharing.

In the culture of the 1960s the attitude toward pre-marital sex and cohabitation was rather carefree. Then, if it wasn't "harmful," an action was deemed permissible, and very few people in authority positions (the Church excluded) saw any harm in the choice of a couple to live together before marriage.

Although there has been some growth in awareness among many in our culture of the Church's teaching on the immorality of sexual intercourse before marriage, this teaching is far from clear to all. It is, as the new *Catechism of the Catholic Church* has stated, "gravely contrary to the dignity of persons and of human sexuality which is naturally ordered to the good of spouses and the generation and education of children" (CCC 2353).

Today, we also have the benefit of a generation of research on the effects of cohabitation. We also have a longitudinal statistical pool of information that suggests that divorce rates among couples who lived together before marriage is higher than couples that did not live together. The reasons for this appear to be found in the very teaching on marriage that the Church has been expounding throughout its long history.

Put succinctly, a lasting commitment requires a mature freedom where a person can speak honestly and forthrightly with his or her partner about the concerns and tensions of the day. Anything that limits this freedom places hidden "strings" on the relationship that implicitly state: "If you raise this issue I might not stick around." The foundational issues, because they have the greatest potential for conflict, often do not get the attention they deserve. One study found that couples who lived together tended to avoid issues such as finances, careers, children, and the like because of the potential negative impact on the relationship.[24]

Thus we can see that cohabitation can actually cause harm to the marriage bond down the line, especially if a deep trust and confidence in the permanence of the relationship has not been formed. A marriage built on withholding of trust and self-surrender does not live up to the ideals of Christ put forth by the Church. There is good reason to be concerned about a couple who lives together.

A Pastoral Approach to Cohabitation

As in any pastoral dilemma the person of Jesus becomes central in finding appropriate solutions. In this case we can turn to the story of "The Woman at the Well" (Jn 4:4-42) for developing an approach that can be helpful. In this story we find Jesus meeting a Samaritan woman at Jacob's well. The two engage in a dialog that sometimes appears to be a sparring match. At one point Jesus tells the woman to "go call your husband and come back" (Jn 4:16). When she replies that she doesn't have a husband, Jesus confronts her honestly and tells her she is correct, that she has had five previous husbands and that the man she is living with now is not her husband. As she becomes aware that this is a man she cannot manipulate, this confrontation becomes the beginning of a deeper conversion for the woman.

Thus, we find that Jesus places the stress on *being honest about what is happening* and on *conversion*. These two points can become the central strategy for anyone working with preparing an engaged couple for marriage.

It does no good for anyone to deny that a couple is living together. The most likely reason for an engaged couple to deny this is fear that they will be refused marriage. This sometimes leads them to a deception of the priest, deacon, or pastoral minister doing initial preparation with them. Most seasoned priests, deacons, and pastoral ministers know from experience that moving the couple beyond fear of judgment and rejection leads to a much deeper dialog about the consequences of cohabitation. Only with such a dialogue, guided by God's grace, can the couple be led to carefully reconsider their situation.

It should be noted that most dioceses have a set of policies and procedures concerning the issue of cohabitation. The priest, deacon, or pastoral minister of the parish most likely knows about these policies and practices and the lead couple or team member who encounters this issue should start first at the local level, the parish, in discovering what approach should be taken. In many cases the priest, deacon, or pastoral minister has already become aware of a couple's cohabitation because of the proximate preparation that has already taken place. More than likely, if any action is to be taken concerning an engaged couple living together this action will be taken by the priest, deacon, or pastoral minister preparing the couple.

What about the issue of a cohabitation when it surfaces in the marriage prep program itself? Here again, the issue is one of honesty that can lead to the deepening of conversion. The following points may help in developing an approach toward this issue.

> 1. Remember your role as a lead couple when this issue surfaces. If a couple confides in you concerning their living situation, it is because they trust you and believe that you will maintain confidentiality. Your role is first to be a mentor, guide, facilitator, and then a teacher. As such, respecting the confidentiality of the engaged couple is important. It is a good idea to ask your pastor before you work with an engaged couple how the issue of cohabitation will be treated and what your role is regarding this specific issue. By respecting the confidentiality of the couple you can do much to dialog with them concerning their experiences and the stance of the Church (See below, #3).

Keep in mind that priests have numerous meetings with an engaged couple before they are sent to a marriage prep program. Chances are the priest is already aware that a couple is living together and that he has already taken steps to address the situation. He might even indicate this to the couple when an assignment is made. It is not your role to ask a couple to make different living arrangements. This is the role of the priest and it is his responsibility to decide how to approach this pastoral situation.

2. If you as a lead couple are uncomfortable with working with an engaged couple that is living together you should discuss this with your parish priest as part of your training to be a lead couple. You need to be informed as to the diocesan policies concerning cohabitation and how they are implemented in your local parish. Before you decide to discontinue working with an engaged couple because you object to the morality of their action, consider that you run the risk of violating the original hospitality that you offered the couple when you began working with them. Consider making this hospitality an evangelical hospitality by continuing to work with them and calling them to a deeper truth at the same time.

3. Above all else, it is incumbent on the lead couple or the team member to "teach as the Church teaches." In discussing some of the reasons why couples live together before marriage Pope John Paul II concludes:

> Each of these elements presents the church with arduous pastoral problems, by reason of the serious consequences deriving from them, both religious and moral (the loss of the religious sense of marriage seen in the light of the covenant of God with his people; deprivation of the grace of the sacrament; grave scandal) and also social consequences (the destruction of the concept of the family; the weakening of the sense of fidelity, also toward society; possible psychological damage to the children; strengthening of selfishness).

> The pastors and the ecclesial community should take care to become acquainted with such situations and their actual causes, case by case. They should make tactful and respectful contact with the couples concerned and enlighten them patiently, correct them charitably, and show them the witness of Christian family life in such a way as to smooth the path for them to regularize their situation.[25]

Thus, the lead couple or team member needs to avoid condoning the behavior, yet also avoid judging the engaged couple so harshly that it drives them away from the community. The most important element that Christian married couples have to offer a couple who is living together is the dual witness of a public commitment and the virtue of joy that flows from the grace of a marriage that was sacramentalized in a public way.

4. A respectful listening to the engaged couple's experience and charitable challenge to try something different seems to be what Pope John Paul II is calling for in the above statement. There are many different reasons why a couple might choose to live together. Listening to a couple concerning these reasons can easily signal a stance of respect on part of the lead couple or team member. Respectful listening can be combined with good, solid reasons why living apart until the marriage occurs could be an invitation to a deepening of maturity on the part of the engaged couple.

5. Keep in mind that the grace of God works in ways that we often cannot see or comprehend. While a couple living together presents a pastoral difficulty, it is also an opportunity for evangelization. The witness of a married couple to an engaged couple living together plants seeds of faith and maturity that may take years to grow into fullness. We often touch people in unseen ways. That is the legacy of faith and grace.

Dealing With Resistance

From time to time a lead couple or team member will encounter a couple or an individual who resists the process and makes it clear that one or both do not want to participate in the marriage prep program. Some behaviors that indicate that there might be resistance happening:

- extended silences, especially after attempts to involve the party have been made by a lead couple or team member,

- frequently passing when it is his or her turn to share,

- consistently answering questions in short, terse sentences,

- letting one's fiancé answer for him or her,

- clear verbal challenges to having to participate in the program,

- disinterested body posture such as: rolling of the eyes, looking away, sighing, foot-jiggling, etc.,

- talking to someone else during presentations, or simply not doing the exercises requested.

What to Do

In most cases resistance can be overcome by directly addressing the behaviors noticed as soon as possible. It is best not to let such behaviors go on too long, as they can become entrenched and begin affecting the participation of other members (if it is a group program) or engender anger on the part of the lead couple or other team members.

Reasons for resistance vary with each couple. The lead couple or team member might want to begin thinking about the following areas when getting ready to address the issue:

• Possible conflict between the couple and the priest, deacon, or pastoral minister preparing them for marriage at the local parish level. Sometimes this preparation does not go well and the couple comes into the sessions angry and expecting the trouble to continue.

• Possible conflict between the two engaged people either as a result of relationship difficulties or as a result of an issue raised by the priest, deacon, or pastoral minister at the local parish level.

• A conflict that arises at the beginning of the marriage prep program. Sometimes personality conflicts begin to emerge where one or both of the engaged parties reacts negatively to either a lead couple or team member. Sometimes there is resistance because a couple does not understand what is expected of them throughout the program.

The following suggestions are given in the hopes of minimizing resistance and dealing with it as soon as it occurs. Again, remember that the more quickly action is taken, the more quickly the facilitation of the session gets back on track. It is up to the lead couple or team member to make the unconscious resistance conscious so that it can be dealt with adequately.

1. In the beginning of the program, whether it be a group program or a couple-to-couple program, someone can invite resistance by saying: "We don't expect you to like everything we do over the course of the program; indeed, you might even have negative reactions to some of the exercises; that's OK. We do want you to be as open as possible to sharing your experiences and reflecting more deeply on your commitment to one another. Also, in your preparation so far you all have had interaction with someone back at the local parish level; by now you most probably have met with the priest, deacon, or pastoral minister preparing you for marriage and perhaps even the musician. In our experience, most of these encounters go well; sometimes, however, there are glitches or conflict over different things that can make some people feel negative. If this has happened to you we want you to be able to talk about this when appropriate, especially if it prevents you from participating fully in this program."

2. Once the program has begun and there is still resistance the best thing is to ask the couple or individual to speak to a team member privately. In the case of a couple-to-couple program this invitation can occur naturally in the room where you usually meet. Keep the focus on the behaviors observed and keep your conclusions tentative. An example might be: "Michael, I noticed that you have been quite silent for this entire session. Is something on your mind that's stopping you from participating?" Allow for the individual to say what he or she is thinking and feeling.

3. If an individual mentions conflict with a priest, deacon, or pastoral minister or with a musician, try to join with him or her by validating the feelings and frustrations. Resist the urge to defend the minister. Your job is to reduce resistance, not to defend the person or the policy. On the other hand, it is appropriate to offer assistance in problem-solving, especially if the couple feels frustrated with the person who is working with them. The best thing to do in most cases is to encourage the couple to talk honestly with the person with whom they are having conflict.

Encouraging the Silent Partner, Working With the Talkative Partner

Whether your program is designed around a couple-to-couple or group format you will encounter from time to time an individual who is much more silent than his or her partner. In cases such as these it is important to assess whether the silence is due to resistance or is more part of the temperament of the individual. One must keep in mind that there is a wide range of relationship styles and that just because a person or couple act and respond differently than you would doesn't necessarily signal a problem. Some people simply prefer not to speak as much as others and will resent any attempt to make them share at a pace at which they are uncomfortable.

Silence rooted in resistance is a different issue from silence that is rooted in one's temperament and personality. In the case of resistance, once the problem is addressed and cleared up, the person usually begins to participate more.

Silence That Signals a More Serious Problem

There is another type of silence that might signal a more serious difficulty, and that is a silence that indicates an individual's passivity in relationship with a partner's apparent dominance or control. Such cases often manifest themselves in an "over-adequate/under-adequate" pattern where one person often speaks, interprets, and acts for the other more silent, passive person. Another characteristic of this pattern is a clear lack of confidence on the part of the quiet partner and a clear confidence and competence on the part of the talkative partner. This type of pattern becomes evident, for instance, when one person is asked a direct question but their fiancé answers for them. Another manifestation of this pattern is when one person always takes the lead in answering and the other person holds back, gives simple yes/no responses, or clearly defers to his or her fiancé.

An over-adequate/under-adequate relationship pattern could signal problems later in the life of the relationship. As anyone in a long-term marriage knows, we change and mature as the years go by, and anything that is unfinished, rigid, or unhealthy about our relationship will eventually have to be dealt with. It is common for therapists to see couples in their office where one party is asking for major changes where he or she wants to move from an "over-under" pattern to more of an "equal-equal" pattern where there is much more equality in sharing of tasks, verbalizing, and assertion.

Clearly, an over-adequate/under-adequate relationship will raise questions for a lead couple or team member. The most important type of response that can be made is a gentle but firm intervention that simply reflects back to the couple the behaviors observed. It is important to let the couple know that you have observed specific behaviors without attaching interpretations of good and bad on these behaviors. Also, one can frame the intervention in a way that roots it in your experience. Thus, an intervention might go something like this: "We have noticed that in the last session that you, Bob, did most of the talking for Sally; in our experience marriage requires a lot of sharing on the part of both people and we're a bit concerned that we're not seeing a lot of that. Sally, is there a reason that you chose to let Bob speak for you this last time?"

Once the issue is confronted and put out in the open many engaged couples will appreciate at least the concern expressed. Many others will address directly the concerns raised as they also want to ensure success in their relationship. Some, however, will become defensive and only acknowledge a small part of the problem. It is best not to get into a control struggle with them, as your role is to prepare them for, not prevent them from, marriage. If, as a lead couple or team member you feel that the problem is a serious one, you can suggest that they talk to the priest, deacon, or pastoral minister who is working with them on the parish level; also you can make a referral to a therapist who is experienced in relationship counseling. This is especially helpful when a couple acknowledges that they have been experiencing problems in this regard.

What to Do With the Talker

Sometimes one party is not necessarily dominant; he or she is simply talkative. This sometimes occurs with people who are very extroverted, but who also have low self-esteem. Talking, or getting connected with others, is a major way for a person such as this to feel OK about themselves and receive feedback. This person might not have a highly developed sense of how he or she is perceived by the group, and can often benefit from encouragement and gentle challenge.

Effective encouragement centers on making it clear to everyone involved that all opinions count, and that everyone is invited to share at least once per exercise. Gentle challenge is needed when the talker breaks the rules and interrupts or intrudes. The leader of the exercise must gently and firmly remind that person that it is not his or her turn yet or that others still need to share. This can be done with humor, especially if trust has developed. Also, it can be said in a way that creates affirmation for the talker as well as others in the group. An example of this could be, "Ken, you have a lot of good things to say, but we also need to hear from the rest of the group (or from your fiancé)."

In summary, keep in mind the following when dealing with a silent or overly talkative participant:

1. When you begin any session or exercise emphasize the rule that you want each person to share his or her response to at least one of the questions or items contained in the exercise.

2. Early on, set the norm for conversation using the Rules for Simple Sharing. (See "Techniques That Enhance Sharing," pages 53-56.)

3. When you encounter a person who is silent make an assessment as to whether the silence is rooted in resistance, temperament, or in a relationship pattern such as the over-adequate/under-adequate pattern.

4. In all cases develop trust and rapport with the silent participant. If the silence is rooted in resistance, be honest with the person and ask for an honest response back in getting at the core of the resistance. If the silence is rooted in temperament, signal acceptance and confidence that this person can communicate his or her needs when necessary.

5. If you determine that the silence is rooted in an over-adequate/under-adequate relationship pattern then prepare to raise this issue with the couple. If this is a group program it is important that this confrontation take place away from the group so that confidentiality can be maintained. If you need help in preparing for such an intervention,

ask someone you trust and who is competent in handling such cases how you might proceed.

6. In dealing with the talkative partner remember to set the norms for sharing early and often. The best remedy in this situation is for the lead couple or team member to set the pace and intervene as soon as the "talker" begins to interrupt or talks too long.

Confidentiality

When an engaged couple comes to a marriage prep program, most are not concerned with whether the material they discuss will be kept confidential. Yet, once they become aware of the issue, most engaged couples will expect that what they say will not be reported back to a parish priest, deacon, or pastoral minister. Thus, we can speak of a general expectation for confidentiality of matters discussed in both the group program and lead couple format.

Many parishes give a lead couple or a group program basic information about the engaged couple. This information may be as basic as street address and phone numbers. In a couple-to-couple program the priest, deacon, or pastoral minister is much more free to discuss with the lead couple information of a more serious matter. For example, a minister might discuss with a lead couple whether a couple is living together and what has been done to challenge this situation. In other cases, special information that is pertinent to the participation in the program might be revealed to the lead couple.

In the case of a group program there is usual little sharing of personal information about the couple. There often is, however, some sharing on the part of the group program leaders back to the parish concerning attendance in the program.

It is important for program leaders and team members to establish right away with the engaged couple how the flow of information back to the priest, deacon, or pastoral minister is going to work. This means that some simple rules need to be worked out between the parish and the people administering the direct service of marriage prep.

Generally speaking, the more confidentiality can be established and maintained, the more trust can be expected to develop; it follows that with greater trust comes greater participation and ownership of the program. Thus, guaranteeing confidentiality—that a program or lead couple doesn't secretly report back to the priest, deacon, or pastoral minister—is a good thing to do.

The following are some simple steps that a program or lead couple can do in establishing the norm of confidentiality:

1. Early in the first session establish the expectations for confidentiality. Say something like this: "It is our expectation that what is said in these sessions are confidential in nature; we do not report back to whoever is preparing you for marriage. If you have a specific difficulty that involves your priest, deacon, or pastoral minister we will listen to you and help you find a resolution to the problem. We won't get involved in any difficulty unless asked, and even then we might decline to get involved."

2. Establish how you will act if a serious problem emerges. You might want to say something like this to the couple(s). "Sometimes a serious issue beyond the normal issues or problems emerges. If this occurs, and we feel that it is a serious threat to your relationship, we will speak with you first about the matter. We might encourage you to speak with whoever is preparing you for marriage, and if you agree to do so, then the matter at our level might be resolved. If we feel that we must speak to whoever is preparing you we will first of all bring this up to you. This type of situation is a very rare occurrence. We want to establish the expectations for confidentiality right off the bat so that there are no surprises down the line."

As with any relationship, establishing expectations and trust is very important. A couple who feels they know what to expect and can trust you to keep your word will relax and begin to own the goals of the program. It is important to be clear with the couple(s) about how it is you will act if a serious problem emerges. A couple who trusts that you will encourage them to first handle the problem will feel that you are treating them like adults.

When Is It Permissible to Break Confidentiality?

There are some difficulties that emerge where a lead couple or team member might feel bound by conscience to speak to the priest, deacon, or pastoral minister, even after saying something to the couple. These issues represent serious difficulties in the relationship and can be generally characterized by the following:

An Indication of Serious and Active Substance Abuse

All of us know that substance abuse is a serious problem in our society and we shouldn't be surprised when an engaged couple manifests a problem in this area. Because of the tendency toward denial over this issue, it is sometimes hard to detect a problem even when there is an active and quite serious difficulty. A person who is dependent on alcohol or another substance can easily mask the dependency or simply deny that there is a problem. He or she can show up at a program sober, for example, yet maintain a dependency by drinking heavily at other times.

48

Sometimes a problem of this sort surfaces during the marriage prep program, and then team members or the lead couple are left with a dilemma concerning whether to speak to the engaged couple. Even though these types of confrontations are difficult to do, it is always best to err on the side of honesty. Simply saying, "N. we have become concerned that you might have a problem with. . . ." is a sufficient intervention to get the ball rolling. It is recommended that if something is said that you also state your intention to speak to the priest, deacon, or pastoral minister about the situation. Any intervention like this should be done with the idea in mind of moving the person or couple into counseling as soon as possible so that the issue can be addressed quickly.

Physical and/or Psychological Abuse

This situation emerges in a public way very infrequently. The most likely people to see the first hints of abuse of this sort will be doctors and other medical providers. A woman coming in for her annual checkup might confide in her doctor that she is in an abusive relationship with her fiancé. But this is an often hidden issue, and is hidden from Church representatives very well, because of the shame, embarrassment, and sometimes threat of physical harm that is associated with the problem.

Nevertheless, it sometimes emerges in a marriage prep program that there is physical abuse present in a couple's relationship. If this does, it is important to construct a strategy carefully. Protection of the person being abused should be the first concern. Some abusers will retaliate against their victims if he or she attempts to break free. The case of physical abuse is one where it seems permissible for a lead couple to discuss their concerns directly with the priest, deacon, or pastoral minister, even before saying anything to the couple. In fact, it might be the best thing not to say anything until a strategy is constructed that maximizes the best possible solution for the couple to get help.

One strategy, after discussing this with the priest, deacon, or pastoral minister, is for the person to speak privately with the victim of abuse and raise the issue with her (in most cases the victim of physical abuse is the woman). The support of the Church can be offered as well as a clear statement that the Church in no way condones an abusive relationship. If addresses of safe shelters need to be given out, that can be done at this time. This strategy allows the priest, deacon, or pastoral minister to assess the relative safety of a person involved in such a relationship.

Once safety can be assured, the priest, deacon, or pastoral minister is in a position to confront the behavior directly and make a referral to counseling. Many men who become physically abusive have themselves been abused, and as long as there is not a pattern of substance abuse present, can be helped in controlling and managing their anger so that the violence is extinguished completely. Certainly, a referral for counseling is in order in this case, and the couple will need to postpone the wedding until the problem is resolved.

It sometimes happens that the issue is one of emotional abuse: the presence of put-downs, belittling comments, criticism, and anger directed toward the other person that clearly suppresses his or her self esteem and spells for trouble down the line. In this case, the lead couple or team member has much more freedom to address this directly to the couple by pointing out the behavior and how it appears to be affecting the relationship. Again, stating that you will contact the priest, deacon, or pastoral minister, if the pattern is seriously harmful, is a strategy that says to the couple that there are certain behaviors that are certain to kill a relationship and may even prevent a sacramental bond from being established in the first place.

In all of the strategies outlined above the main goal is not to punish or embarrass but to raise hope that a better relationship is possible if the couple is able to confront the harmful behavior and willing to seek professional help. While these confrontations are seldom pleasant, they serve as a witness of honesty and truthfulness that the Church will not deny real problems when they surface.

The Unity Candle

At first glance it would seem that a topic such as the Unity Candle should not be part of a marriage preparation manual. After all, the topic of the unity candle belongs more properly to the details of planning for the actual wedding ceremony. But because it is becoming a contentious issue in wedding planning, it is quite possible that the engaged couple will actually raise this issue.

The unity candle itself is a relatively recent phenomenon, having developed in the last twenty years or so. It is not used in all Catholic parishes, and more and more dioceses are beginning to develop policies restricting the use of the candle, and even prohibiting the candle from being used during the actual wedding ceremony. This, of course, often causes frustration in the couple preparing for marriage, especially if they had plans to use the candle.

The unity candle itself is simply a candle shaped in such a way that there are three distinct wicks. Two of the wicks are on the periphery of the candle and are lit before the ceremony begins. Sometime after the vows are taken the couple goes to the unity candle and each lights a taper from one of the already lit wicks. Together they light the middle wick, symbolizing the new unity of the "two become one."

Some parishes permit the unity candle; others do not. A couple expecting to use the candle in the ceremony can be quite upset if their particular pastoral minister refuses to allow it. They might then carry this conflict into the marriage prep program and express anger at the priest, deacon, or pastoral minister.

The reason that some parishes do not permit the unity candle to be used has to do with the potential confusion of what symbolic action constitutes a sacramental marriage. Some pastors and theologians hold strongly to the view that since the spoken vows of the man and woman bring about the sacrament, nothing should obscure this symbol. They fear that the unity candle may begin to dominate and overshadow the symbolic action of the spoken vows and eventually begin to be seen as the true symbol of marriage.

Others, of course, feel that the above objections do not hold much sway and that the unity candle is a relatively harmless addition to the liturgy that further symbolizes the notion of the "two become one." Without taking a stand as to what is right or wrong, it is important for the lead couple or team member to be aware that this might be a potential area of conflict between the engaged couple and the parish. While it may appear to be a small thing, it is usually the "small things" that explode to create large conflicts.

Just serving as a listening and friendly ear can go a long way in helping diffuse any anger and tension over an issue such as this. Be careful, however, not to serve as an intermediary for the couple, since your role is not defined this way. If there is a problem, it exists between the engaged couple and the pastoral minister with whom they are working. You can listen sympathetically and offer suggestions that encourage the couple to either accept the situation or talk again to the pastoral minister. In some cases you may be able to help the couple understand the reasons behind such a decision. Whatever the outcome, this may be a valuable opportunity for the couple to hear clearly, and for the first time, the theology of marriage that emphasizes their role as serving as ministers of the sacrament by speaking their vows publicly. If nothing else, the couple may at least feel a deeper pride at knowing that marriage is the only sacrament where the ministers of the sacrament are the two people receiving it.

5

Techniques That Enhance Sharing

The following techniques are presented with the understanding that the lead couple or team leader may already possess a great deal of knowledge and experience concerning how to facilitate sharing between people. These techniques should be taken for what they are: techniques. In reality it is the leadership of the lead couple or marriage preparation team that is most responsible for meaningful sharing. Your energy, enthusiasm and willingness to assist in the preparation of an engaged couple for marriage is in itself helpful in facilitating dialog. The following techniques are meant to compliment the accumulated experience and wisdom that you bring to the task of facilitating preparation.

The Good and New

Desired Outcome: Beginning a session that emphasizes the positive in people's lives while allowing everyone a chance to share.

Best Used: In the beginning of a session to gather the group.

"The Good and New" is an exercise that can be done with two to ten couples, depending on the time available.[26] The goal of the exercise is to build rapport and a positive mindset among participants. This exercise is meant to be done quickly, with little comment from participants.

The exercise consists in having each person in the group say one thing that has been "good and new" for him or her since the last time the group met. It is best to simply move around the circle giving each person ten to twenty seconds to tell the group their "good and new." Of course, as with any exercise, if a person does not wish to participate he or she can simply say "pass."

Sharing of Personal Symbols

Desired Outcome: Deepening of trust and sharing within a group based on the sharing of personal symbols. This exercise often facilitates in-depth sharing of personal stories.

Best Used: After the group has achieved some cohesiveness and when people feel more trust in the group; usually around the third or fourth session of any process. It can also be used at the beginning of any couple-to-couple session. This exercise can also be used at the last session to bring the entire program to a close.

"Sharing of Personal Symbols" is an exercise where people are asked to bring with them a personal memento that has given meaning to their lives. The setting for this exercise can be informal or ritualized. In an informal setting people sit in a circle and simply take turns explaining to the group the meaning of their symbol. In a ritualized setting there may be a quiet time for music, then a time for people to light individual votive candles, place them on a table or altar, then speak about the personal meaning of their symbol.

In this exercise, if comments are given when people share their symbols, they should be affirming and positive. Some examples of symbols that may be shared are pictures, engagement rings, jewelry given by parents or grandparents, poems, photographs, memorabilia from an important time in one's life, etc.

This exercise easily can be adapted during the session on children by having everyone bring one or two photos from their own family of origin. Then, to begin the session, participants share their photos, telling stories from their own experience. In a group program, couples should break up into small groups for sharing. In a couple-to-couple program the sharing takes place between the lead couple and the engaged couple.

The Whip Around

Desired Outcome: Checking in with what people are thinking or feeling about a given session; allowing people to give feedback quickly and succinctly.

Best Used: At the end of a session to do a quick evaluation and/or to assess the impact of the session on a person. Sometimes used after a more serious discussion, or where there is a lot of silence that is confusing to the facilitator.

"The Whip Around" allows for the group to give feedback on a specific question that is given to them by the facilitator or team. The benefit of this exercise is that it allows for everyone in the group to say either how they were affected by the session or to give specific feedback on a particular question. It is always best to have the question in mind that will be asked of the group. The facilitator poses the questions and then tells the group that they will "whip around" the circle and give each person about twenty seconds to respond to the question. Remember, as in all group exercises, individuals must be given the option of passing. In the case of a marriage prep group, whether it be a large group or a just a lead couple and engaged couple, some of the questions can be phrased this way:

• As a result of this session, one thing I will either work on or be aware of this week is. . . .

• One thing that I learned about myself tonight is. . . .

• One thing that I learned about my fiancé is. . . .

The Group Within a Group

Desired Outcome: Enhancement of listening by a large group, especially where there is increased tension and/or stereotypes that need to be challenged without creating animosity.

Best Used: When there is a need to allow certain opinions and feelings to surface without being challenged immediately. This exercise will take from forty minutes to an hour.

"The Group Within the Group" is a good technique to use in a group between twenty to fifty members. It consists of having an outer ring and an inner ring. The group can either stand or sit depending on the length of the exercise. In a group of around twenty people there might be six people in the inner circle and fourteen in the outer circle. One way to use this exercise in a marriage prep setting is to have a representative group of women sit or stand in the inner circle. They are told to begin a discussion among themselves about a specific topic. For instance, they might be asked what they want to see happen when they have conflict with their fiancé's. Each member of the inner group is told that when she has spoken her mind that she should go to the outer ring. Other women from the outer ring, when ready to speak, come into the circle and say what they are thinking. No one on the outer circle is allowed to comment.

After a period of time the facilitator asks if there are any more women in the outer circle who want to share. If not, then a representative group of men are asked to go into the inner circle and they are asked to respond to the same question. The process goes on until every man who wants to share has been given an opportunity to share. Then, the circles are joined into one big circle and there is processing of what people heard, the commonalities shared between men and women and the differences.

Rules for Simple Sharing

Desired Outcome: Making listening the norm for every session and activity within each session. Also, slowing down the "talkers" while encouraging the "non-talkers" by a method that everyone agrees to.

Best Used: Whenever there are small group discussions where the goal is to allow everyone in the group to say at least one thing they are thinking or feeling.

The "Rules for Simple Sharing" represent a process where small groups can run efficiently yet not fear being dominated by one or two people. These rules require an introduction the first time they are used and work best when they can be given as a handout. It is necessary to remind people about the rules each time they get into groups until the entire group has internalized the rules and can do the process easily and without resistance. The rules are as follows:

1. Each person in the group is asked to share one thought or feeling on the topic at hand. The group will not be successful unless everyone has been given an opportunity to share.

2. When someone shares, other group members can only ask clarifying questions about what was said. An example of a clarifying question is: "Are you saying that . . . " or "What did you mean when you said . . . " People are asked to refrain from giving their opinions about another person's sharing.

3. Each person is asked to adopt a stance of openness and tolerance for the opinions or statements of others in the group.

4. People are given the option to pass when it is their turn to speak; everyone is encouraged, however, to say something on the topic at hand.

5. Once everyone has been given an opportunity to share, people are asked to go around the circle again, this time commenting on what they heard other people say.

6

Facilitating the Sessions

The Flow of the Sessions

This manual has been prepared keeping in mind that the people who implement the material often make adaptations to the material in their planning and in the actual unfolding of the sessions. The sections in the participant's booklets are designed to be modular in application. This recognizes that program leaders and lead couples often make pastoral decisions to adapt whatever program they are using to meet their own needs. It is hoped that the person implementing each session views the session notes as only one way of implementing the session; it is acknowledged that there are often various alternatives to implementation on the local level.

Each session has been designed for a time frame of between two and two-and-a-half hours. The author will leave it up to the individual to implement a longer or shorter program by combining modules and by picking and choosing from the material present. *It is strongly recommended, however, that any adaptation include the section entitled "Faith at the Heart of Your Marriage" as well as at least one of the case studies.*

It is far easier to implement a couple-to-couple program in that the group dynamics are pretty straightforward: most couples start from the beginning of the material and take a leisurely route from beginning to end. Since there are only two people to plan for, the lead couple has the luxury of more time for each person and need not worry about the complexities of group dynamics.

For those engaged in a group, notes are included under the heading "Group Program." For those who are engaged in a couple-to-couple program there are implementation notes under the heading "Couple-to-Couple." In planning a group program there is a need to follow a schedule. Approximate times for implementing each section are given, listed after the heading introducing each section.

For those implementing a group program there are more complex group dynamics to consider. Sometimes, you will want to have small group reflection. At other times you will want to have the engaged couples spend time alone with the material. And finally, if you plan on having any "witness talks" by married couples, you will need to factor this into your planning. It goes without saying that there will be more than enough material to occupy a two to two-and-a-half hour session, since the more participants there are, the longer it takes to complete exercises and make the transition from one activity to another. For anyone involved in a group program, there are implementation notes under the heading of "Group Program."

Most of the implementation notes will concern specific suggestions on the material. From time to time there will be comments listed in italics which will cover a more general topic such as covenant or sacrament. The comments are meant for both Group and Couple-to-Couple Programs. Keep in mind that the most important element of any effective marriage prep program is the witness and participation of the lead couple or team member. The material is meant to facilitate a dialog and bring the engaged couple to a deeper understanding of their commitment and love for one another. When all is said and done, a newly married couple will remember the people who helped prepare them, not the book they used.

SUGGESTED OUTLINE

Session One: Building Your Marriage on a Sound Foundation

Total suggested time: 2 hours, 55 min–3 hours, 5 min

Comment: *Because of time constraints, you may need to allow less time for some of the sections. Another possibility is to leave a section for the couple to do at home on their own. This will become a necessity if you plan sessions that run for just two hours. For instance, you may choose not to do a section in favor of having a group discussion on one of the case studies. It is recommended that you give enough time for the material on the spirituality of marriage, even if you do not cover all of the material.*

1. Welcome and Greeting of Couples (5 min)

2. Opening Prayer and Overview of Program (10 min)

Group Program: Use the prayers in the couple's book or have a team member design a prayer service.

Couple-to-Couple: Use one of the prayers in the back of the book, a memorized prayer such as the Our Father, or a spontaneous prayer offered by either member of the lead couple.

3. Sections 1 & 2: Energy, Excitement & Gifts We Give (15 min)

Group Program: Have the couples spend time going through each section, answering questions. Then, have each couple pair with another. Each person is to share his or her answer to one item from each section.

Couple-to-Couple: Give the couple time to complete the sections, then ask them to respond to each question one by one or only to the questions that interest them.

4. Sections 3 & 4: Your Expectations & Great Expectations (15 min)

Group Program: Have the couples do the exercise; then fiancés are to share with each other their responses. The positive expectations that the Church has for an engaged couple's marriage can be stressed in the talk later in the program.

Couple-to-Couple: Have the couple do the exercise on their own expectations. Feel free to raise the issue of the Church's expectation for their happiness and lasting commitment. This might be a good time to stress the covenant relationship that frames the marriage commitment. See the section "A Sacred Covenant, a Holy Sacrament" on pages 32-34.

Comment: *This is a good time to break the stereotype of the Church as the stern parent ready to reprimand the person who steps out of line. Emphasize with the couple(s) the high hopes and earnest prayer for joy and happiness that the Church has for them. In the group program this can be addressed through the presentation/"witness talk;" in the couple-to-couple program this can be addressed in the normal course of the conversation.*

5. Section 5: Realistic Expectations? (30 min)

Group Program: Have the couples go through these expectations and fill out their responses. Then, divide them into small groups of no more than six people to a group. Ask each person to share a response to at least one question to which he or she responded.

When dividing couples into small groups, you may want to review the rules for simple sharing. Also, the issue of unrealistic expectations can be addressed in a presentation or "witness talk."

A budget sheet is provided in conjunction with this section for couples to do on their own.

Couple-to-Couple: After the couple finishes this section allow them to go through the expectations at a leisurely pace. Make sure that your personal disclosures from your own marriage facilitate the sharing of the engaged couple. It is appropriate and helpful to talk about how you dealt with your own unrealistic expectations, but be careful to allow the engaged couple to speak, too. If they are eager and excited to share, try to keep them talking.

A budget sheet is provided in conjunction with this section for couples to do on their own.

Comment: *Expectations can create ambivalence on the part of a couple getting married. On the one hand, expectations tell us something about the future we want; on the other hand they can become an obligation that we rebel against. As the couple(s) share(s) on this material be sensitive to any tension surrounding expectations that one or both feel are unattainable or unrealistic. This may be harder to monitor in a group format; if it does occur be ready to offer any couple discreet but appropriate counsel. Often, couples need to be reminded that tension over expectations is a normal part of a committed relationship. Look for especially troublesome expectations such as the expectation that marriage will change another's drinking or harmful conflict resolutions style (name calling, hitting, etc.). These call for a different sort of intervention. (See the section on "Confidentiality," pages 47-50.)*

The desire to change one's spouse is perhaps the biggest stumbling block that trips up a couple early in marriage. It is especially important to address the expectations of each spouse in this area.

Also, be sensitive to how a couple appears to handle conflict. Some of this may begin to surface in the first session. Don't be surprised when you discover that some couples are more open to dealing with anger and conflict. "Anger" and "conflict" are two words that many of people don't connect to a healthy marriage. Yet research indicates that as anger and conflict are dealt with and resolved, a marriage is made stronger. It is when anger and conflict are avoided and replayed again and again that real difficulty is created.

6. Speaker/"Witness Talk" (15 min)

Group Program: This is a good place to have a "witness talk" from someone who has had to adjust his or her expectations in the course of his or her marriage. This topic can be joined with the notion of "covenant relationship" where there exist both realistic and unrealistic expectations. It is best to make such a talk as experiential as possible while placing stress on how spirituality helped the speaker adjust to the reality of being married. It would be ideal if this presentation could be made by a couple, with each spouse briefly offering his or her own perspective.

7. Break, Group Program only: 10 minutes maximum

8. Sections 6 & 7: Building on Solid Ground & Twelve Foundational Factors (40 min)

Group Program: This next section is crucial in helping the engaged couple understand that spirituality is holistic, that it includes the entire person. Encourage the couple to see their own religious beliefs and practices as extending into their everyday work week, their time alone and with their friends. Have the couples complete this section in quiet. Then send each engaged couple away to talk privately with each other. Have them report back after thirty minutes.

Couple-to-Couple: Think carefully about how you might present the idea of a spirituality of married life in a positive and interesting way. Where appropriate, speak about your experience concerning what your own faith and spirituality has meant to your marriage. Also, in your own marriage, which foundational factors were fully present at the time of your marriage and which ones did you need to develop through the course of your marriage?

Comment: You may want to facilitate discussion by asking the couple to identify three or four foundational factors that they have either not thought about or that impress them as especially important.

Another approach if time is running short is to have the couple(s) simply check the factors where they think they are doing well, and put a (-) sign next to those factors where they wish to improve. You can then encourage the couple(s) to look at the questions sometime in the following week.

9. Case Study (20 min)

Group Program: Divide the couples into small groups of not more than six people. Assign them one of the case studies and ask them to read it, answer the questions, and then discuss the case.

Couple-to-Couple: Try to leave enough time to discuss at least one of the case studies. Have the couple read through the other case study and answer the related questions during the next week.

Session Two:
The Two Will Become One

Total suggested time: 1 hour, 40 min–2 hours, 5 min

Comment: *Because of time constraints, you may need to allow less time for some of the sections. Another possibility is to leave a section for the couple to do at home on their own. This will become a necessity if you plan sessions that run for just two hours. For instance, you may choose not to do a section in favor of having a group discussion on one of the case studies. It is recommended that you give enough time for the material on the spirituality of marriage, even if you do not cover all the material.*

1. Opening Prayer (10 min)

Group Program: Use the prayers in the couple's book or have a team member design a prayer service.

Couple-to-Couple: Use one of the prayers in the back of the book, a memorized prayer such as the Our Father, or a spontaneous prayer offered by either the lead couple or engaged couple.

2. Section 1: Faith at the Heart of Your Marriage (10 min)

Group Program: Introduce this section by stating that beginning with the second session, the couples will start with a short reflection on the spirituality of marriage. Have the engaged couples take time to read over the section. Then, ask each couple to share their answers with each other for five minutes.

Couple-to-Couple: After checking in with the engaged couple, mention that each session from now on will begin with a short reflection on the spirituality of marriage. Next, ask the couple to read over the section and then answer the questions. Then, have them choose one or two responses to share with you.

3. Section 2: Knowing Yourself (20 min)

Group Program: Have each person take five minutes to do the exercise. Then, break into small groups of two or three engaged couples. Each person is to share one thing they checked about themselves. Everyone is asked to share at least one thing before anyone shares another item. Let this process continue for fifteen minutes.

Couple-to-Couple: Invite the couple to take five minutes to do the exercise. Then ask them to begin sharing. Some engaged couples want to know as much as possible about the other person and will want to go through the items one at a time. Other couples might want to jump around. Simply ask if either of them wants to begin the sharing; let the couple determine the pace. Intervene by asking questions only if there are long silences.

Comment: Sometimes there is some awkwardness concerning sharing, especially in the beginning of any group. If this appears the case you might want to try out the "Good and New" exercise in the future. (See page 53.) This exercise gives a simple way to break the ice without taking a lot of time. If you use this exercise in a group format ask the small groups to begin with it. In a couple-to-couple approach this exercise can be used right after the opening prayer.

4. Sections 3 & 4: Family of Origin's Influence & Factors Which Form Relationships (25 min)

Group Program: Have each person take 10 minutes to read through the material and fill out his or her responses to the ten factors. Then, divide into small groups again, asking each person to share one factor that they marked "low" and one that they marked "high." It is important to remind the groups of the rules of simple sharing, since some people may feel vulnerable in their sharing.

Couple-to-Couple: Have the couple read through the section and make their responses to the exercise. Then work with them through the material. A follow-up question to ask both of them is: "Are there any factors in particular that you want your partner to be aware of as you begin a life together?" You may want to share with the engaged couple where the two of you were with the ten factors when you were first married.

Be sensitive to the fact that this exercise might encourage a deeper story telling on the part of the engaged couple. It's OK to get "side-tracked" and take longer with the material, especially if it facilitates a deeper sharing between the two.

Comment: One's family of origin can be both a great resource and a great burden. This fact often gives rise to the state of ambivalence in that a person experiences a "love-hate" relationship with his or her family. This is true even for people who come from families that are relatively intact and psychologically healthy. Just separating and becoming independent from one's family of origin can create a powerful emotional reaction. On the one hand a person is excited to be on his or her own, while on the other hand he or she might miss the warmth and protective structure that the family once provided.

All of this becomes more complicated when we consider how many people come from families that are more seriously dysfunctional. Many people, for example, have experienced a family environment that was either overly intrusive or neglectful.

*Even when a person experiences these negative influences, however, there is still a tendency to be loyal to one's family. When an engaged couple begins to share their experiences with others it is important to note that they might **minimize** any negative influences while **idealizing** positive ones. This may cause a lead couple or team member to feel that a participant is not being completely honest, but it's important to remember that people tend to share more deeply as they begin to trust more. If you encounter any resistance in this exercise remind yourself that as the couple begins to develop a deeper trust and rapport, their sharing will most likely deepen.*

5. Break, Group Program only (10 min)

6. Section 5: Blending Your Approaches (10 min)

Group Program: This section will be done in two parts. The first part is to be done before the witness talk, the second part involves a discussion of the material after the witness talk. Allow the participants time to read the material and then go through the exercises. Tell them that this is preparation for the talk, which will recount one couple's experience of how they blended the various aspects of personal habits, friends, work, and social interests.

Couple-to-Couple: It will be helpful to share your own experience of having blended personal habits, friends, work, and social interest into your early married life. Give the couple time to go through the material and complete the exercises. Then, move through the material at a leisurely pace, sharing your own experiences when appropriate. Remember, your personal disclosure is meant to facilitate a deepening of sharing and trust. Be careful not to dominate or talk too long when you share. Personal disclosure is especially helpful when the engaged couple comes to an issue where there is obvious tension or where they feel stuck. Your sharing can help to reassure them that difficulties can be worked through.

7. Witness Talk, Group Program Only (15 min)

Group Program: The witness talk, if included, can address one couple's experience of blending the various interests outlined above. This talk can be delivered by a couple or by one spouse. Again, it's best if the speaker(s) can make realistic connections to a spirituality of marriage as it relates to this topic.

After the witness talk is finished put the couples into small groups of two to three couples. Ask participants to share one or two items from the exercises in Section 5; they can also address issues and themes from the witness talk they just heard. Keep in mind the rules of simple sharing. You may have to remind the couples about the importance of having everyone share at least once.

8. Sections 6 & 7: Marriage as Journey & Constructing Your Timeline (30 min)

Group Program: Have the engaged couples read over silently the material in this section and construct their timeline. Then, have the engaged couples spend time alone sharing the results of their individual timelines. After a suitable time bring them back together. Ask for a few volunteers from the larger group to respond to the following questions:

Did you learn anything new about yourself as a result of doing the timeline? Did you learn anything new about your fiancé as a result of this exercise?

Couple-to-Couple: Allow time for the couple to read through the material and complete the timeline. Then, have them share their results in a leisurely fashion. Ask the same question given in the paragraph above.

Comment: This may be a good time to ask the couple to re-read the introduction to the couple's workbook since it has an imaginative journey based on the gospel passage, "The Road to Emmaus" (Lk 24:13-35).

9. Case Study (20 min)

Group Program: Divide the couples into small groups of two to three couples. Assign a case to each group. Allow a few minutes for individuals to read the case and respond to the discussion questions. Have the small groups focus on their answers to the questions following each case.

Couple-to-Couple: Ask the couple to select a case, read it over, and respond to the reflection questions. Then, facilitate a discussion of the case.

SUGGESTED OUTLINE

Session Three: Establishing Emotional and Sexual Intimacy

Total suggested time: 2 hours, 15 min–2 hours, 40 min

1. Opening Prayer (10 min)

Group Program: Use the prayers in the couple's book or have a team member design a prayer service.

Couple-to-Couple: Use one of the prayers in the back of the book, a memorized prayer such as the Our Father, or a spontaneous prayer offered by either the lead couple or engaged couple.

2. Section 1: Faith at the Heart of Your Marriage (10 min)

Group Program: Everyone is asked to read over this section and respond to the reflection question that follows. Then, each engaged couple is asked to process how each person responded for five minutes.

Couple-to-Couple: Give time for the couple to read over the material and answer the reflection question. Then allow for processing of each person's responses.

Comment: The notion of a sacrament as an efficacious sign that points to a deeper reality rooted in Christ may be familiar to someone raised in a Catholic family. But to others it may be totally new. Keep in mind, too, that many couples share an interreligious experience. One person in the pair may be Protestant, Jewish, Muslim, or may profess no belief whatsoever. It may be a good idea to be ready at least to pursue the notion of sacramentality a bit more deeply if the couple indicates interest. For reference, see Chapter 3 "Understanding the Sacrament of Marriage."

3. Sections 2 & 3: Emotional Nurturing and Intimacy & What Is Intimacy? (25 min)

Group Program: Have the participants spend time reading over the material in Section 2 and answer the questions that follow. Then, have them go on and complete the exercise in Section 3. After everyone has completed these two sections divide the couples into small groups of no more than three couples. Invite each person to share at least one response from Section 2. Then, after everyone has shared at least one of their responses, have the groups go on to share responses from Section 3. After the groups have concluded, in the large group, ask for two to three responses from the engaged couples on the following questions:

Did any of you learn anything new concerning how your fiancé defines intimacy?

Did you learn anything new concerning what is easy for your fiancé to offer you when you're hassled or upset? What is difficult?

Couple-to-Couple: Have the couple take time to read over Sections 2 and 3. Then, ask them to respond to the reflection questions following Section 2. Be ready to follow up when an individual states that he or she has changed as a result of falling in love with his or her fiancé. Most of these changes will be for the better. It will be a rare occurrence when a person states that knowing his fiancé has made him or her worse off. If this occurs this may be a sign of trouble and you need to be ready to pursue this. (Refer to the section on "Confidentiality," pages 47-50, for help in this regard.)

After participants have shared their responses to Section 2 ask them to respond to Section 3. Be ready to ask follow-up questions. See the questions given above for the group program.

4. Section 4: What's Love Got to Do With It? (20 min)

Group Program: Introduce this section by stating that the couples will be asked to look at three different components of married love. Have them take time to read the material and then respond to the two questions that follow. Then, break the large group into small groups of not more than three couples and ask the participants to share their responses.

Couple-to-Couple: Have the couple take time to read through the material in this section, then to answer the questions that follow. Feel free to share with the couple how your percentages have changed throughout the history of your relationship. For instance, you may have had a great deal of "love as feeling" early on in your relationship only to re-define this when your children began to arrive and you had less time to spend on the feeling aspects of your relationship.

Comment: *This section makes some important distinctions concerning what we mean by married love. There is, of course, a popular notion of love as passionate, intense feeling for the other, popularized in the music of the "top 40." The only problem with this notion is that it cannot sustain a marriage when the feeling begins to fade. Married couples who have been together several years realize that there needs to be something more than just feeling. This is where love as committed stance and process of intimacy comes into play. It is important to stress with the engaged couple the necessity of these other two forms of love. It is hoped that the engaged couple will see that love is not just a given in their relationship but that it is also something that can be worked at and created again and again.*

5. Break, Group Program only (10 min)

6. Witness Talk, Group Program Only (15 min)

Group Program: The witness talk, if included, can be one person's (or one couple's) experience about how intimacy was and is created in the marital relationship. It can draw material from the previous sections about how often men and women take the expectations of the other for granted. We think we know how to meet the needs of our spouses without really checking out our assumptions with our spouse. A talk such as this might also focus on the third aspect of married love, that of love as a process of growth, reconciliation, forgiveness, etc. that creates a lifetime of intimacy. A couple or individual can address how their notion of love changed to include a continual process of communication, forgiveness, etc. Finally, time can be given to highlighting the National Conference of Catholic Bishops' criteria for developing a mature conscience in the area of sex and sexuality.

7. Section 5: Rules for Intimacy (15 min)

Group Program: This section follows easily after a witness talk, especially if the talk addresses the creation of intimacy within a marriage. Have the couples read through this section and respond to the "intimacy rules" listed, checking the appropriate responses. Then, break into small groups of not more than three couples. Have each person in the group share at least one thing that is easy for them to do and one thing that is difficult for them to do from the exercise; have them share any other "rule" that they have listed at the end of the exercise.

Couple-to-Couple: Have the couple fill out their responses to this section. Then, ask them to go through the material together giving their responses to what is difficult and what is easy for each of them to do regarding intimacy.

Comment: This might be a good time to gently suggest that all of us from time to time need to turn to an outside source, like a priest or therapist, for help when our relationship begins to bog down. Intimacy is easier to sustain in the beginning of a relationship and it can be sustained and deepened throughout the relationship if a couple takes the time and energy to foster it. Keep in mind that 50% of the marriages that fail in the United States fail within the first seven years. This tells us that many couples do not weather the first early crisis of intimacy and communication.

8. Sections 6 & 7: Exploring Sexual Love & Taking Responsibility for Married Love (15 min)

Group Program: Have the couples read through the material from these two sections and complete the exercises. Then, split the individual engaged couples up so that partners can discuss their answers to the exercises privately. Explain to them that it is important that they have a common understanding of and clear expectations for sexual intimacy. Ask them to pay close attention to any areas where there are clear disagreements. When they come back together again as a large group, if there is time, this may be a good time to clarify any questions regarding Church teaching on this subject.

Couple-to-Couple: Have the couple go through the two sections and respond to the exercise. Tell them that if there is any area that they do not wish to discuss with you that you will respect their wishes. Stress with them the importance of a common understanding of and clear expectations for sexual intimacy. Your role as a lead couple is to serve as a facilitator and resource to them. It is hoped that by the third session enough trust is developed between you and the engaged couple that they can share freely their responses.

Comment: The section "Exploring Sexual Love" contains the National Conference of Catholic Bishops' criteria for the development of a mature conscience in the area of sex and sexuality within marriage. It is a good idea to point these criteria out to the couple(s) so that they realize that the Church's teaching on sex and sexuality is based on an articulated theology of the human person. Another reason for noting these criteria is that many couples may be surprised that they actually agree with the criteria, and that they have had misconceptions of the Church's teaching based on media accounts, which often portray an overly simplistic notion.

9. Section 8: Marriage as a Conversation (20 min)

Group Program: Allow for time to read through this section and for each person to give his or her response to the exercises and questions. Then, break into small groups of not more than three couples. Have each person share one thing he or she is doing well with, one thing he or she wants to improve on, and one response to the reflection questions at the end of this section.

Couple-to-Couple: Allow for time to read through this section and invite the couple to do the exercises that follow. Then, ask them to name one or two items where each is doing well and one or two items where each wants to improve. Have them also give their responses to the reflection questions.

10. Case Study (20 min)

Group Program: Break the large group into small groups of not more than three couples. Assign each group a case study and allow enough time to read through the case study and answer the questions. Then, ask each person in the group to share at least one answer to the reflection questions. Make sure that the groups remember the rules of simple sharing, and that everyone feels that they can share at least one response. Remember, cases can be given as "homework" if you don't have enough time to get to them.

Couple-to-Couple: Ask the couple to choose one of the case studies, read through it, and answer the questions. Then, ask them to share their response to the case study. If you have enough time, go on to the next case. Remember, case studies can be given as "homework" if you don't have enough time to get to them.

SUGGESTED OUTLINE

Session Four:
A New Family Circle

Total suggested time: 2 hours, 15 min–2 hours, 40 min

1. Opening Prayer (10 min)

Group Program: Use the prayers in the couple's book or have a team member design a prayer service.

Couple-to-Couple: Use one of the prayers in the couple's book, a memorized prayer such as the Our Father, or a spontaneous prayer offered by either the lead couple or engaged couple.

2. Section 1. Faith at the Heart of Your Marriage (10 min)

Group Program: Have the couples take time to read the short section and give their responses to the questions. Have each engaged couple pair up with another engaged couple to go through their responses. By now the couples should have developed enough trust to share on the level of faith and spirituality.

Couple-to-Couple: Have the couple take time to read the short section and give their responses to the questions. Then, take them through their responses. Be ready to have them react to the quote, "You can fire an employee, but you can't fire a family member."

3. Sections 2 & 3: How Were You Parented? & Your Family Position (15 min)

Group Program: Introduce this exercise by stating that it is time to get in touch with how our families have influenced our formation. Have them fill out the exercise and then break into small groups of no more than three couples. Remind them of the rules of simple sharing and have each of them share the characteristics that he or she checked along with the responses to the two reflection questions. *This is also a good place to have couples share one or two photos from their own family of origin. See "Sharing of Personal Symbols" page 54.*

Couple-to-Couple: Have the couple complete the exercise and the two reflection questions. Then, invite each to share the characteristics he or she checked along with the responses to the questions. *This is also a good place to have couples share one or two photos from their own family of origin. See "The Sharing of Personal Symbols" on page 54 of this manual.*

Comment: The way we are raised exercises subtle yet real influences on us. Not only our parents, but also our siblings, give us behavioral criteria for our selection of a mate. For instance, a male raised in a family where all his siblings were male might have a more difficult time later on in life understanding the needs of his wife, especially if his relationship with his mother was distant or conflictual. Another married man, later in the marriage, might realize that he didn't "marry his mother" as much as he "married his sister."

4. Section 4: Parenting Styles in Your Family of Origin (15 min)

Group Program: Have the couples take time to complete the two exercises on parenting styles. Then, have them pair up with another couple to share their responses. Tell them to be sure to cover the reflection questions at the end of the section, since it is possible that many of the participants experienced a blend of two of the three styles of parenting.

Couple-to-Couple: Allow time for the couple to go through the exercises in this section and to consider the follow-up question. Have them share their answers. Place emphasis on the fact that their responses represent their experience, and that there are no "right" or "wrong" answers.

Comment: Our experience of our family of origin can bring up a great deal of ambivalence. On the one hand we tend to be loyal to our families; on the other hand we may also have some unresolved issues with our parents that bring up feelings of frustration and anger. Be ready to reassure the participants that these exercises are not about assigning blame or expressing anger, although that may occur. Rather, the purpose of these exercises is to allow the participants to reach a level of awareness that may move them to resolve any unfinished business, thus allowing them more freedom in their future relationship with their spouse.

5. Section 5: Your Parents' Disciplinary Techniques (20 min)

Group Program: Ask the couples to read through the material and respond to the exercise. Then, divide the couples into groups no larger than three couples. Have them share their responses to the exercise and the following reflection questions. Ask them to be aware of the rules of simple sharing and put stress on sharing the reflection questions, as these questions point them toward their future as parents. Stress with all the couples the importance of honoring someone's decision to pass and not share, since this material can evoke powerful memories that some people do not want to process in this type of setting.

Couple-to-Couple: Ask the couple to read through the material and respond to the exercise. Be aware of the fact that this material can evoke deep emotions, especially if a person has experienced a negative form of discipline such as shame. Preface the sharing by stating that if there is any material that each person does not want to share, this will be respected.

Comment: It may be a good idea to have ready a few names of therapists and family counselors that can help someone sort through the power of their family of origin. If you notice someone upset or especially quiet this may be an indication that the material has struck a deeper, more conflictual chord with that person. The sessions themselves are not an appropriate vehicle for therapy, but a lead couple or group leader can go a long way in encouraging a person to resolve issues that are unfinished.

6. Break, Group Program only (10 min)

7. Witness Talk, Group Program only (15 min)

Group Program: It's recommended that a witness talk done by either one person or a married couple serve as a bridge between the material in the first half of this session and the last half. A talk should cover the speaker's experience of having been formed by his or her family and how that formation affected the early years of marriage. Then, the talk can lead into how his or her family of origin experience shaped the early years of child rearing, including pregnancy, childbirth, and the transition period that followed.

8. Section 6: Becoming a Parent (15 min)

Group Program: Allow time for everyone to fill out this exercise. Then, ask each couple to pair off with another couple. Ask them to share their responses to the checklist, and their responses to the hopes and fears they have as they imagine bringing children into the world.

Couple-to-Couple: Allow time for the couple to fill out the exercise. Then, ask them to share their responses. This may be a good time for you to share some of your own experiences; when the couple describes something that scares them, for instance, you can reassure them by admitting

74

that the same thing was scary for you (assuming it was, of course). Pay particular attention to the hopes and fears that they have as they imagine bringing children into the world.

9. Section 7: Marriage as Growing a Garden (30 min)

Group Program: Have the couples read through the material and respond to the reflection questions. Then, have each of the engaged couples spend time by themselves processing the material. After about fifteen minutes of processing the reflection questions, bring them back to the large group to discuss their responses with everyone. Pay particular attention to the group's response to the notion of baptism. Stress that the Church wants to be an active part of their lives not only when they marry but when they have children as well.

Couple-to-Couple: Allow time for the couple to read through the material and respond to the reflection questions. Then, ask them to share their responses to the questions.

Comment: Don't be afraid of silences. Sometimes couples might find it difficult to share on the topic of spirituality. This is because generally we are not used to talking about our faith and spirituality on a daily basis. Thus, a couple might fall silent when faced with more serious questions about their spirituality. Be comfortable with silence. Remember, just about everyone feels awkward when there is silence. If you can keep silent longer, chance are an engaged person will break the silence and begin sharing. Then, you're off and running!

10. Case Study (20 min)

Group Program: Break couples into small groups of not more than three couples. Assign each group a case study and ask them to spend five minutes reading over the case and answering the questions. Then, ask each person to share his or her response to at least one of the questions.

Couple-to-Couple: Have the couple select which case they want to discuss and then read through it silently. After they have read the case, have them write their answers to the reflection questions. Then allow for discussion.

SUGGESTED OUTLINE

Session Five: Dealing With Conflict

Total suggested time: 2 hours, 5 min–2 hours, 40 min

1. Opening Prayer (10 min)

Group Program: Use the prayers in the couple's book or have a team member design a prayer service.

Couple-to-Couple: Use one of the prayers in the couple's book, a memorized prayer such as the Our Father, or a spontaneous prayer offered by either the lead couple or engaged couple.

2. Section 1: Faith at the Heart of Your Marriage (10 min)

Group Program: Have the couples read through the material and give their responses to the reflection questions. Then, have each couple pair up with another couple and discuss their response to this section.

Couple-to-Couple: Invite the couple to read through the material and give their responses to the reflection that follows. Don't forget to give your own reaction to the material.

3. Sections 2 & 3: Our Response to Conflict & Getting in Touch With Your Conflict Style (20 min)

Group Program: Explain to the couples that this session will cover not only the way we think and respond to conflict, but that it will also involve practicing new ways of resolving conflict. Ask the couples to read through the section and then do the exercise that follows. Then, break the couples into small groups of not more than three couples. Have them share their responses to the checklist as well as the reflection questions.

Couple-to-Couple: After explaining the purpose of the session (see above) have the couple take time to read the material in the section and complete the exercises that follow. Then, take them through the material, being sensitive to the questions on family of origin.

4. Section 4: Conflict Resolution Begins With Clear Communication (25 min)

Group Program: This next session introduces material concerning how we communicate with each other. Invite the couples to read through the section. When they are finished, summarize the material on pages 96-98, emphasizing the percentages of verbal, voice tonality and body posture that are actually listened to. Then, invite the couples to answer the reflection questions on page 98. After they have done that ask each engaged couple to discuss with each other their responses to these questions.

Couple-to-Couple: Have the couple read through the material in this section. Then, have them answer the first reflection question on page 98. Begin by asking them if they find anything surprising in this material (pages 96-98). Also, ask them if the pattern of "feel, think, do" makes sense to them. Be prepared to give an example from your own experience. Then, go on to the final question about the block to listening. Ask each person to give their response to this question.

Comment: Listening is an art form that is taken for granted. The tendency is for us to read the other person's mind and assume that we know what he or she is going to say in advance. In marriages that have failed, respondents indicated that poor communication and conflict resolution skills ranked high on the list of factors that led to the marital breakdown. It makes sense to practice some skill-building, but the trouble is that when communication is practiced it often becomes artificial and feels forced. You may receive some resistance from participants over this; if so, use the above information as a way of persuading the participants that it is in their own best interest to take a look at more effective communication and conflict resolution skills.

5. Sections 5 & 6: Requests of the Other & Good Communication Takes Practice (20 min)

Group Program: Introduce these sections by stating that the following section gives a model for communicating clearly and directly with another person. Give the participants time to read over these two sections. Then, have them focus on a positive event that happened in the past week, completing the exercise in Section 6. After they have done this, pair the couples up. Have one couple act as an "observer couple" and the other as the "communicating couple." Each person is asked to communicate the positive event to his or her fiancé; after each couple has done this they are to receive feedback from the "observer couple" whether they were clear in describing the event, their feeling-reactions, the consequences, their thoughts, and what they want in the future.

Couple-to-Couple: Allow the couple time to read through the material and complete the exercise in Section 6. Then, act as the "observer couple" and invite each person to share their communication of the positive event that occurred this past week. Give the couple feedback on how clearly they described the event, their feeling-reactions, the consequences, their thoughts, and what they want in the future. Be ready to use examples from your own marriage to make clear the benefit of direct communication.

6. Break, Group Program only (10 min)

7. Witness Talk, Group Program only (15 min)

Group Program: This is a good time to consider having a "group within a group." See page 55 of this manual for details. Place six chairs in the middle of the room and arrange all the other chairs around the outside so that there is a large outer circle and a smaller inner circle. Invite four married people to take the circle on the inside. Ask them to begin to talk about times in their lives when they resolved conflict successfully, and what obstacles must be overcome in resolving conflict. Before the exercise begins tell those on the outer circle that whenever they have a question or comment they can come into the inner circle and take one of the empty chairs. After they have asked their question and received an answer, or after they have made their comment, they can return to the outer circle.

Another variation to this exercise is to have a small group of women take the inner circle and then discuss some of the more difficult aspects to resolving conflict. Then, a small group of men are asked to take the inner circle and discuss the same question.

After the discussion goes on for ten or fifteen minutes, ask everyone to move to the outer circle. Ask those who were quiet for their reactions and observations regarding the exercise. Ask if anyone learned anything new about conflict and conflict resolution.

8. Sections 7 & 8: Knowing How to Fight Fairly & Conflict Checklist (15 min)

Group Program: The list entitled "Conflict Rules" has a step-by-step process that couples can follow when faced with conflict. There are two choices that can be made concerning the couples' practicing these steps: they can either practice during the program or you can assign this as something to work on during the week. In any case, invite them to read the rules and then follow the directions underneath the rules.

Next, give the couples time to go through the conflict checklist (Section 8). Then, break them into small groups of not more than three couples. Have each person share his or her response to at least one item.

Couple-to-Couple: Make a decision as to whether you will have the couple process the "conflict rules" during the session or later during the week. If you defer to later during the week make sure that the couple understands how to complete the exercise. Next, ask them to go through the conflict checklist, giving their responses to the statements. Then, have them share all of their responses or the ones that strike them the most.

Comment: There are some particularly harmful ways of communicating that can worsen conflict and inflict fatal harm on a relationship. According to John Gottman,[27] constant criticism, "stonewalling," contempt and constant defensiveness are four serious harmful factors that can destroy a relationship. Also, explosive rage and/or violence should be taken as a warning sign. If anyone gives an indication that any of these factors exist in their relationship it might be a good idea to consider making a referral for counseling. Sometimes people will make joking reference to negative ways of communicating and conflict resolution; this could be an indication of a more serious underlying issue. On the other hand, many people bring into marriage a mixture of healthy and unhealthy ways of relating.

9. Section 9: Marriage as Friendship (20 min)

Group Program: Have the couples read through the material and respond to the exercise and question. Then, have each engaged couple spend time alone sharing their responses with each other.

Couple-to-Couple: Have the couple read through the material and respond to the exercise and question. Then, have them talk about the responses they listed. Be ready to share your experience concerning how you grew together as friends.

10. Case Study (15 min)

Group Program: Break couples into small groups of not more than three couples. Assign each group a case study and ask them to spend five minutes reading over the case and answering the questions. Then, ask each person to share his or her response to at least one of the questions.

Couple-to-Couple: Have the couple select which case they want to discuss and then read through it silently. After they have read the case, have them write their answers to the reflection questions. Then allow for discussion.

SUGGESTED OUTLINE

Session Six: Facing Change and Keeping Your Foundation Intact

Total suggested time: 2 hours, 15 min–2 hours, 40 min

1. Opening Prayer (10 min)

Group Program: Use the prayers in the couple's book or have a team member design a prayer service.

Couple-to-Couple: Use one of the prayers in the couple's book, a memorized prayer such as the Our Father, or a spontaneous prayer offered by either the lead couple or engaged couple.

2. Section 1: Faith at the Heart of Your Marriage (10 min)

Group Program: Invite the couples to read over the section and then respond to the reflection questions that follow. Then, ask the individual engaged couples to spend time giving their responses to the reflection questions.

Couple-to-Couple: Invite the couple to read over the section and respond to the reflection questions. Then have them share their responses. Be ready to share how the two of you have balanced individual and couple volunteer work.

3. Section 2: Change Happens (20 min)

Group Program: Have the couples complete the exercise on change. Then, have each engaged couple pair with another and share how they responded to the exercise.

Couple-to-Couple: Have the couple complete the exercise on change. Then, invite them to share with you their responses to the exercise.

4. Section 3: Something Lost . . . Something Gained (20 min)

Group Program: Introduce this section by stating that important changes often require us to face leaving something behind while gaining something important. Read through the first two examples of "loss and gain," and then invite the couples to read through the rest of the material. Invite the couples to complete the exercise described in the text. Next, divide couples into small groups of no more than three couples per group. Ask each person to share one change with his or her small group (two if there is time). Make sure that participants know they have a right to pass if they feel the change listed is too personal to share.

Couple-to-Couple: Take time in going over the first two examples of change in this section with the couple. Then, invite them to read this section and reflect on the exercise that is described in the text. When they are ready, ask each of them to share his or her responses with you. Be ready to share significant changes from your married life.

5. Section 4: Are You Stressed Out? (15 min)

Group Program: Ask the couples to complete this next section on stress. Where the checklist provides a space for "other," have them consider wedding planning as a stressor. After they complete the exercise, allow time for individual couples to process the results together.

Couple-to-Couple: Ask the couple to complete this next section keeping in mind the above suggestion that wedding planning can be a significant stressor. After the couple has completed the exercise have them share their responses. Also, be ready to share with the couple the times in your own marriage when the two of you had to deal with the impact of stress. Make sure, however, that you do not dominate and take away from the couple's own processing of the stress that they currently experience.

Comment: *Relationships often are the first victims of a life lived under high stress. The symptoms of burnout and depression are surprisingly similar: loss of concentration, sleep disturbances, over- or under-eating, irritability, fits of anger, feelings of desperation. Many marriages are negatively affected just by the fast pace of life, workplace anxiety, and the like. Even a "simple" thing like wedding planning can cause such stress in us; it is a known fact that engaged couples often experience increased tension and arguing as the wedding day approaches.*

Your role as a lead couple or team member may be simply validating that an engaged couple's stress is on the rise and helping them understand that this is a very normal occurrence. Sometimes an engaged couple will disclose that they (or at least one of them) are under an extraordinary amount of stress. For instance, an engaged person might have a close friend or relative with a serious illness, or be dealing with a serious job issue at the same time he or she is preparing for the wedding. In this case be ready to provide a sympathetic ear. Often just naming his or her stress is enough to allow a person to feel more in control of their fast paced days.

There are, of course, healthy and unhealthy ways to deal with stress. If a couple shares that there is an increase in alcohol consumption it may be important to pursue this and ask for more clarification. Certainly, there is a difference between a sustained pattern of alcohol abuse and drinking as a reaction to increased stress. The feelings of the person who has noticed this behavior are crucial. It is important to stress that drinking to relieve stress can be harmful to the relationship without implying that the behavior is necessarily "alcoholic." It may be important to suggest getting an assessment from a qualified alcoholism counselor if the behavior is clearly an issue. See the article on Confidentiality for a more thorough discussion on drinking.

6. Break, Group Program only (10 min)

7. Witness Talk, Group Program only (15 min)

Group Program: This is a good time to have someone address the aspect of change throughout the course of a relationship. A speaker can address the issue of how one changes and develops personally, and the impact that this can have on one's relationship with one's spouse. There are other changes to consider as well: the effect of job loss, relocation, health difficulties, etc. on the relationship. Make sure that you do not make this presentation a "litany of bad things" that can happen in a relationship. Rather, model hope and resiliency to the couples so that they understand that change does not necessarily have to have negative consequences.

8. Sections 5 & 6: Caring for Yourself and Your Relationship & Developing Rituals of Intimacy and Re-Creation (25 min)

Group Program: Allow time for the couples to complete the exercises in these two sections. Then invite each couple to pair up with another engaged couple. Ask them to share at least one thing that they do to care for themselves and one unhealthy way they care for themselves when they are under stress. Then, ask them to share with each other the rituals of intimacy and caring that they have identified in the final section.

Couple-to-Couple: Allow time for the couple to complete the exercises in the next two sections. Then, invite the couple to share their responses to how they care for themselves both positively and negatively. Also invite them to share with each other how they want to create rituals of intimacy and care. Don't forget to share with the couple what each of you do to take care of yourselves and what you do together to enhance and deepen your relationship.

9. Section 7: Holiness Is Wholeness (20 min)

Group Program: Invite the participants to read through the section and then answer the reflection questions that follow. Then, divide the couples into small groups of not more than three couples per group. Ask each person to share their response to the questions. Remind them of the rules of simple sharing and suggest that they might want to take the questions in sequence so that each person has a chance to say at least one thing.

Couple-to-Couple: Allow time for the couple to read through the section and answer the reflection questions that follow. Then, invite them to share their responses to the questions. Be ready to pick up on the questions involving suffering since it is more than likely that each person will know someone who has suffered a great deal for no apparent reason. Also, when they mention the couple that they admire be ready to probe as to what it is about that couple that makes them a model of resiliency.

Comment: The question of suffering is perhaps the hardest and oldest question asked of religious systems. It challenges our expectations and assumptions about what life is all about. Many of us have positive expectations of the future and are not prepared for the bad things that can come so suddenly.

This raises the larger question of what it means to be holy in today's world with its many demands and unseen dangers. Even if we don't suffer major tragedy, we are pulled in many diverse directions by the demands of our jobs, children, and other relationships. Given this reality, Jesus' call to not worry about our future can seem to be idealistic and naive. Yet, it also can seem to be grounded in a very deep wisdom, that ultimately it is God who is in charge of the universe.

10. Case Study (15 min)

Group Program: Break couples into small groups of not more than three couples. Assign each group a case study and ask them to spend five minutes reading over the case and answering the questions. Then, ask each person to share his or her response to at least one of the questions.

Couple-to-Couple: Have the couple select which case they want to discuss and then read through it silently. After they have read the case have them write their answers to the reflection questions. Then allow for discussion.

Alternative First Session for Couples Who Are Planning Remarriage

In the course of marriage preparation it happens from time to time that a parish priest will refer a couple contemplating remarriage to either a marriage prep lead couple or to a marriage prep program. This assumes, of course, that the couple contemplating remarriage has done what is needed to secure a declaration of nullity, if necessary.

While a separate program for those planning remarriage is perhaps the most helpful solution, a priest or parish administrator may not have access to a fully developed program. Thus, adaptation is often the best solution.

When working with a couple preparing to remarry it is important to assess the type of marriage prep work that is needed. Someone who was married for twenty years, divorced, and is now contemplating remarriage will have different needs from someone who married in their late teens, divorced after only a year or two of marriage, and is now remarrying in his or her early to mid-twenties. In the first case, it may be appropriate for the pastoral minister preparing the couple to work with them individually, adapting the program to meet their needs. In the second case, having the couple go through a complete marriage prep preparation seems to be the appropriate thing to do.

Some dioceses have separate, distinct programs to address the needs of people who remarry. In this case, making a referral to such a program is certainly a choice of the pastoral minister who works with the couple.

Recommendations for adapting this program to the needs of couples remarrying: The best and simplest approach to adapting the program is to have the couple begin with Session Six, **Facing Change and Keeping Your Foundation Intact,** with a few modifications. Below are specific questions that the couple can start with. These questions will help the couple to address what went wrong in their first marriage, how each has changed as a result of the failure of the first marriage, and what each has learned about themselves as a result of the failure of their first marriage. Also included below are two specific case studies which address the situation of a couple facing remarriage.

After answering the questions below the couple can then go on to complete the rest of Session Six, utilizing the case studies as a way of addressing further their unique situation. This adapted sixth session can be done with a marriage prep lead couple or with the pastoral minister who is working with the couple at the local, parish level. After the adapted session is completed, a decision needs to be made as to whether further sessions are required. If so, the couple can be asked to complete the remainder of the sessions with a lead couple or be referred to a group program. The ideal situation would be for the couple to work on the local, parish level on an adapted Session Six and then be referred to a program designed specifically for couples preparing for remarriage.

Alternative Reflection Questions for Couples Who Are Remarrying: Session Six

1. A breakup of a marriage is almost always conflictual and painful. Yet it is important for you to understand the patterns at work that led to the break-up of your first marriage. What do you believe were the most important factors in the break-up of your first marriage?

2. Looking at your own maturity level at the time, was there anything about your behavior or personality that led to serious problems developing in your first marriage? If so, how have you taken responsibility for your part in the failure of your first marriage?

3. Do you have any deep or lasting wounds as a result of the failure of your first marriage? For instance, some people may have a more difficult time trusting their present spouse because their first spouse was unfaithful. Others might have an underlying anger that suddenly flares if their present spouse does anything to remind them of previous difficulties with their ex.

4. What have you learned about yourself as a result of going through the dissolution of your first marriage? How have you changed?

5. If there are children involved from a previous marriage, has it been easy or difficult to work out things like visitation and child support? More importantly, do you experience any tension over children from your previous marriage(s), either because of differences in the way you discipline or because of difficulties in developing a positive relationship with them? If so, what have the two of you done to insure that this tension is resolved and doesn't stand in the way of creating a solid bond with each other?

Alternative Case Studies:
Session Six

Case One

Rhonda and George were in their early 30's when they first met. Each had been divorced for three years. George had been married for four years and did not have any children. Rhonda had been married for ten years and had two children, ages seven and nine. They hit it off with each other immediately and within a few months began to talk about marriage.

But there were difficulties in their relationship. Rhonda was very sensitive to George drinking any alcohol. This was because her first husband had a drinking problem that only got worse in the years they were married. Even though George did not abuse alcohol, Rhonda became tense and agitated when he would drink at parties, or when they went out together. This led to tension between them; George resented being compared to Rhonda's ex-husband. He continually told her that he was different and felt that Rhonda didn't trust him.

Another issue that created tension between the two was the difficulties that George experienced with Rhonda's children. He had some difficulties with the way Rhonda disciplined them (she was the custodial parent). He felt that she was too lax and allowed them to manipulate her into letting them stay up late and avoid doing their chores. Once, he intervened and disciplined her oldest boy when he called his mom a name. Rhonda felt that George had overstepped his boundaries and told him so. For his part, George felt that her children didn't listen to him and were a bit afraid of him. Whenever they talked about this issue, both of them became defensive and stopped listening to the other.

Reflecting Together

1. Do you think Rhonda was overreacting to George's drinking? Is this a problem that could potentially damage their relationship? What would you advise this couple to do?

2. Concerning the issue of children from a previous marriage, do you think there are any principles governing how this situation should be handled? What is your own experience in this regard?

Case Two

Dan and Judy have been married for five years. Each had been previously married, Dan for eight years and Judy for three. Dan has one child by his first marriage, a boy of age three. Judy has no children by her previous marriage. Dan and Judy met while both were divorcing and took much comfort and solace in each other's company. Their courtship was intense, slowed down only by the length of each of their divorce proceedings. Nine months after the last divorce was granted they were married civilly.

In the five years since they have been married Dan and Judy have had one child. When their daughter turned four Judy began to think about religious education for her child. She and Dan began talking about seeking an annulment so that their marriage could be blessed by the Church. Together they approached their parish priest who began working with them on the necessary paperwork.

In the course of his work with them the priest discovered that there was unresolved tension surrounding their courtship, divorce, and remarriage. It came down to this: Judy and Dan had slept with each other while still married to their first spouses. From time to time Dan found himself not being able to trust Judy's commitment to their marriage, despite her protests to the contrary. Since his first wife had been consistently unfaithful to him his own ability to trust was low. Even Judy's looking at another man at a social function could set off his insecurity.

The priest who was working with them determined that both of them had the maturity and potential to make the marriage last, but that they needed to deal with the unfinished business of their previous marriages. He told them that he would continue to work with them on the annulment but asked them to attend couple's counseling so that they could resolve the issues that sometimes got them stuck in hurt and anger.

Reflecting Together

1. Is it possible that Dan and Judy married too soon after divorcing? Why or why not?

2. What unfinished business do you bring from your previous marriage(s)?

Prayers for the Engaged
and
Newly Married Couple

For a Passionate, Creative Love

Lord, Send out your Spirit
and renew the face of the earth.
Father, Jesus gave his life
because he loved deeply and completely.
May our love for one another
be all encompassing and all consuming.
Make our love be pleasurable.
Make it be creative as it is stable,
passionate as it is respectful,
gentle as it is strong,
so that all who know us will see in our
love the hand of our Creator God.
And when you bless us with children
may they grow in the knowledge of the
passionate and energizing love that
has its beginning in the love you have
for the world and all its peoples.
We ask this through Jesus, our Lord and brother.
Amen.

A Prayer for Understanding

Lord, help us to always seek first to understand each other,
to lead with compassion,
to walk a while in the other's experience.

Help us walk the road of marriage together,
trusting that when we doubt you will give us faith,
that when we criticize you will give us the courage to seek and give forgiveness.

Make our love for one another burn in our hearts
in tough times as well as in the easy times.
May your Spirit renew our love again and again
so that we may give witness to your saving presence in our lives.
Amen.

A Prayer for Perseverance

Lord Jesus, in the garden of Gethsemane
you did not want to face the pain you knew would happen to you.
Yet you persevered and did not run from
what lay ahead of you.
Guide us gently to face our fears.
Like your disciples in the storm-tossed boat
we sometimes feel swamped by life's indifferent pressures.
May your presence always comfort us and lead us beyond fear to hope.
Help us to develop confidence in our own skills;
let us face our future with confidence in your sustaining presence.
Amen.

A Prayer to Tobias and Sarah

Tobias and Sarah, pray for us as we begin a life together.
You risked your reputation and your lives
for the sake of your love for each other.

Keep us faithful to our own journey of love.
Guide us to do what is right, not what others say is right.
May we be helpmates and partners to each other
and may God's Spirit keep us single minded in our fidelity.
May your spirit teach us about energy and zeal for God's love;
as we walk our journey together may God's love always energize us.
Amen.

To Anna and Joachim: On Children

We pray that our children will reach their full potential in the eyes of God,
as did your daughter Mary,
mother of Jesus our Lord.

May God's Holy Spirit lead us in the way of wonder and love
so that when we become parents
we will provide a home full of care, comfort, and structure.

Teach us to be a family that is holy,
one that sees in every person the dwelling place for God's Spirit.
As you taught your daughter Mary,
teach us to value our children for who they are,
not so much for what they can do.

May God keep us always loving and present
to the many joys, struggles, and hopes that our children possess.
Amen.

For Forgiveness: A Prayer to St. Peter

Peter, who Jesus called Rock,
you know the pain and agony of having denied your friend and master.
Yet you were forgiven and called to mighty deeds.

Peter, you were married when Jesus called you to leave your nets and follow him.
Was your wife your silent partner?
Did she anchor you to reality when you dreamed wild schemes
and plans for the newborn church?
Did you have to seek her forgiveness for the excesses of your enthusiasm?

Pray for us, Rock of the church,
when we fail our commitments
and even betray our friendship with each other.
Help us see that beyond the hurt and pain lies the grace of renewal.

As Jesus forgave you
may we forgive each other and not harbor lasting resentment.
May our attitude always be as a child
who quickly forgets the hurt
because of the consoling presence of a loving friend.
We ask this through Jesus, our Lord and brother.
Amen.

A Prayer Concerning Conflict

Jesus, were there ever times when you became angry with your friends?
When you rebuked Peter and called him "Satan"
were you angry because he tried to control what you were saying?

Show us that conflict can be holy ground,
that it need not be destructive.
Keep us honest and respectful of each other when we fight.
Lead us to take responsibility for our words and actions.
Remind us that we can always do better,
especially if we hit below the belt by name calling and harsh criticism.
Above all else, send us your Spirit
to lead us in the way of respect and honesty,
so that our love may continue to deepen through the years.
Amen.

A Prayer to Abraham and Sarah

Abraham and Sarah, you risked all to journey to a new land you did not know.
And when you were old and beyond your child bearing years
God granted your wish for a son.
You dared to dream, to laugh, and to hope in the promise of God.

Pray for us as we begin our journey of love.
Give us some of your vision.
May our dreams be rooted in the passion, perseverance, and humor
that the two of you possessed.
May God always lead us into our future.
Amen.

To Sarah, on Laughter

When the angel announced to Abraham
that you would bear a son,
you laughed because you were old and beyond your years.

Yet God laughed with you and gave you Isaac.
We pray that our marriage be for us a place of safety and a place of mirth.
May God keep our commitment to one another strong
and our love ever growing.
May we be able to laugh at ourselves
and not take ourselves too seriously.

With the help of the Spirit
may we transcend our limitations and sinfulness.
As we grow older we pray that we, too,
can laugh and play in God's presence.
Amen.

The Covenant of Our Marriage

Lord God, you are creator of all things
and you renew our commitments even when we fail
to keep our end of the covenant we make with you.

Keep us faithful to the covenant we enter together.
Help us realize that your sustaining presence
will guide us through the tough times that we will face.

When we are tempted to turn away from each other
help us face our fears.
And when we want to blame the other for not meeting our needs
teach us to take responsibility for ourselves.

Help us celebrate and proclaim
the lasting quality of our commitment to each other,
so that in seeing our love
others may see your presence.
Amen.

The Prayer of All Christians

Our Father,
who art in heaven,
hallowed be thy name;
thy kingdom come;
thy will be done
on earth as it is in heaven.
Give us this day our daily bread;
and forgive us our trespasses
as we forgive those who trespass against us;
and lead us not into temptation,
but deliver us from evil.
Amen.

Endnotes

1. "Introduction to the Rite of Marriage," *The Rites*, Pueblo Publishing, New York, 1990, paragraph 7.

2. Ibid., paragraph 5.

3. *Familiaris Consortio*, Office of Publishing Services, United States Catholic Conference, Washington, D.C., 1981, paragraph 66.

4. *Marriage Preparation in the Catholic Church*, Center for Marriage and Family, Creighton University, November 1995, p. 27.

5. *Familiaris Consortio*, Office of Publishing Services, United States Catholic Conference, Washington, D.C., 1981, paragraph 73, p. 81.

6. *Faithful to Each Other Forever*, National Conference of Catholic Bishops, Washington, D.C., 1989, p. 60.

7. Ibid., p. 60.

8. Ibid., p. 61.

9. Champlin, Joseph M. *The Marginal Catholic*, Ave Maria Press, Notre Dame, Indiana, 1989, pp. 138-139.

10. *Faithful to Each Other Forever*, National Conference of Catholic Bishops, Washington, D.C., 1998, p 62. See also: *Code of Canon Law*, c 1077.

11. Ibid., p. 151.

12. Ibid., p. 40.

13. Ibid., p. 60.

14. Ibid., p. 63.

15. *Marriage Preparation in the Catholic Church*, Center for Marriage and Family, Creighton University, November 1995, p. 46.

16. Pennock, Michael F. *This Is Our Faith*, Ave Maria Press, Notre Dame, Indiana, 1998.

17. Driedger, Pamela. *The Church: Our Story*, Ave Maria Press, Notre Dame, Indiana, 1999.

18. "Introduction to the Rite of Marriage," *The Rites*, Pueblo Publishing, New York, 1990, paragraphs 1 and 2.

19. *Catechism of the Catholic Church*, Liberia Editrice Vaticana, paragraph 1617.

20. *Faithful to Each Other Forever*, National Conference of Catholic Bishops, Washington, D.C., 1989, p. 78.

21. Ibid., p. 78.

22. Ibid., p. 78.

23. Ibid., p. 71.

24. Ibid., p. 73.

25. *Familiaris Consortio*, Office of Publishing Services, United States Catholic Conference, Washington, D.C., 1981, paragraph 81.

26. See Kline, Peter and Bernard Saunders. *Ten Steps to a Learning Organization*, Great Ocean Publishers, Arlington, Virginia, 1993, p. 61.

27. See Gottman, John. *Why Marriages Fail or Succeed*, Fireside, New York, 1994.